Meadow in the Sky

Meadow in the Sky

A History of Yosemite's Tuolumne Meadows Region

Elizabeth Stone O'Neill

Upper Tuolumne Valley from Soda Springs looking south

Panorama West Books

Fresno, California

First Printing 1984
Second Printing (Revised) 1986

Published by
Panorama West Books
2002 North Gateway, Suite 102
Fresno, California 93727

Manufactured in the United States of America

Dedicated to the memory of
Claire Linnaea O'Neill
and to her happy days in Tuolumne Meadows

Old bridge by Soda Springs.

CONTENTS

ACKNOWLEDGEMENTS

In writing this book I have had the help of many knowledgeable people. I would like to express my thanks to Dr. Mary Hill of San Francisco State University for going over the geology chapter; to Yosemite Park Indian Specialist Craig Bates and to Dr. Michael Moratto, both of whom read and commented on the Indian sections; to David Gaines of the Mono Lake Committee, who checked the material on birds; to Dr. Carl Sharsmith, who gave special attention to the geology and botany; to Dr. William A. Douglass of the University of Nevada Basque Studies Program, who read the chapter on sheepherders; to Evelyn P. Wiggen, who shared her recollections of François Matthes; and to Lee and Dorothy Verret, who shared their memories of Tuolumne Meadows with me.

Additional thanks go to Yosemite Park Superintendent Bob Binnewies, David Gaines, Henry Berrey of Yosemite Natural History Association, Chief Park Naturalist Leonard McKenzie, Dr. Walter Payne of the University of the Pacific, Catherine Rose, Dr. Carl Sharsmith, and Yosemite Research Librarian Mary Vocelka, each of whom read the entire manuscript.

All of the above made helpful corrections and suggestions, and share the credit for what merit the book may have, but not the responsibility for errors which may still remain.

There are others too numerous to mention who gave me clues to follow and unexpected bits of information and insight, especially many members of the park staff who answered my questions with unfailing courtesy and care. Mary Vocelka helped in finding historical material and pictures, and constantly encouraged me. Dr. Carl Sharsmith ("Carl" to all of us in the meadows) enriched my appreciation and understanding of that special world on many a hike and climb. And of course, how can I express my debt to those no longer alive who appear in the book, and without whose writings it would have been impossible?

Limitations of space and/or information mean that inevitably the names of a number of people whose life histories crossed that of the meadows do not appear here. My apologies to them.

My most heartfelt appreciation is for my husband, Carroll, who introduced me to the Sierra, shared with me the joy of innumerable mountain days, read and considered the manuscript more times than anyone else, helped and encouraged me, and donated his photograph for the cover, which commemorates some of the best days of our lives.

Finally, my thanks go to Steve Emanuels, Doris Ruebel Hall, Keith Bennett, and all the people at Panorama West Books who took a manuscript and made it into a book.

INTRODUCTION

This book came to be because of an ending. In 1976 the National Park Service closed the walk-in campground at the Soda Springs. Benches and tables were removed, fireplaces were razed and raked clean, and one sunwarmed hillside of Tuolumne Meadows returned to forest. Not a bad thing, one might say. Yet for me, and I am sure for many others, a deep sadness arose at the thought that this historic spot, site of so much history and of so many happy personal memories, was being shut down.

There was still the Parsons Memorial Lodge, but it was shuttered and locked, a forlorn reminder of bygone days. How many an evening I had spent there, reviewing with like-minded companions the pleasures of the day's hiking and climbing and planning hikes and climbs to come!

After knowing the lodge for thirty years, I suddenly began to wonder how it came to be in the first place. Who was Parsons to be so memorialized? Why was it built *here*?

Days spent in the Yosemite National Park Research Library (with the friendly help of librarians Steve Medley and Mary Vocelka) gave me some answers. From the pages of old Sierra Club Bulletins, from yellowed letters and manuscripts, Parsons emerged as a real person. He became one of my comrades on the trail, one of the honored ghosts of Tuolumne Meadows.

My article, "Parsons Memorial Lodge," was published in *Sierra* in September, 1978. Meanwhile, the lodge was reopened. But this was only the beginning. I wanted to know more. I wanted to meet the other ghosts who walked what I egotistically thought of as *my* trails in *my* mountains.

More days and months of research and interviews brought them slowly to life, like long-silent tree spirits now released and walking about in my mind. Soon for me Tuolumne Meadows was peopled with Indians and miners, scientists and dreamers, rangers and climbers for whom they were *their* meadows, *their* trails. I had become infinitely rich in unseen companions.

I had come, too, to appreciate more fully and deeply the meadows I had known for much of my life: their great age, their beauty, their fragility. And to become more achingly aware of what I like to call their meaning.

This book is the result. I hope that through it you will share with me the joy of the mountains and of those who have loved them. May it signify for you not an ending, but a beginning.

ILLUSTRATIONS

View of Tuolumne Meadows from Lembert Dome.

1

FIRST THERE WAS A MEADOW

Tuolumne Meadows lies 8,600 feet high in the sky of Yosemite, not far from the eastern entrance of the national park at Tioga Pass. Those who have seen it once come again and again.

There are other meadows in the Sierra, and all are entrancing, Crabtree and McClure, Colby and Evolution, Little Pete and Big Pete, to name only a few. But Tuolumne Meadows is the queen of the lot. Pete Starr, who wrote *The Guide to the John Muir Trail and the High Sierra Region*, which has been a bible to several generations of hikers, rightly called it "this most beautiful of all high Sierra meadows."

It's about twelve miles long including the Lyell Canyon, and in many places at least a half mile across. The mountains that rim it stand back so they can be seen: Ragged Peak, White Mountain, Dana, Gibbs, Mammoth Peak, Johnson Peak, the Unicorn (which really has three horns), the Cockscomb, Echo Crest and Echo Peaks, Cathedral Peak, Fairview Dome, Pothole Dome. Each has its own shape and character and, from the top, its special view.

Through the meadows flows a river whose two parents, the Lyell and Dana forks, bubble down from the bases of their respective mountains. The Dana Fork is limpid. When the Lyell glacier is melting fast, the Lyell Fork is opalescent; when clear water predominates, as it does most of the time, it is wonderfully clear, pale, golden. They meet to form the Tuolumne, a stream of many moods.

It flows through the meadows and then tumbles downhill in a series of elegant cascades including Waterwheel Falls, grinds out the awesome mile-deep Grand Canyon of the Tuolumne River, and dies as

1

a wild river behind the prison walls of O'Shaughnessy Dam.

Lower down it carves another canyon through the foothills, and is again impounded, this time in the Don Pedro Reservoir. Now almost at sea level, it falls upon evil days in the Central Valley, where it is bled for irrigation and sullied with pollution. Finally what is left meets the San Joaquin and flows out the Golden Gate into the sea.

But our business is with its youth, and with its home territory, Tuolumne Meadows.

It's not a single meadow, but a whole series running the length of a broad basin and following the river. And because of its size, and its nearness to an opening in the eastern escarpment of the Sierra, it has seen more human history than any other High Sierra meadow. From Indians to miners and sheepherders, from homesteaders to naturalists and rangers, and today's backpackers and tourists—whatever of note people have said or thought or done about the Sierra, much of it happened here.

It was not always a meadow. Geologists are still trying to piece together the story of the Sierra; the picture they now present goes something like this: Long, long before the glaciers—about half a billion years ago—this sea of peaks was a sea of water. There countless generations of marine creatures lived and died and were gathered into sediments of sand and mud which grew thicker and thicker until of their very weight they turned to stone.

Then, starting about 200 million years ago and continuing for about eighty million years, deep in the earth under this sea was a huge up-welling of granitic material which formed a gigantic underground dome, the core of the Sierra. This Great Sierra Batholith, as it is called, kneaded, twisted and changed the over-lying sediments to metamorphic rock, as it slowly lifted them into the sky.

Now a period of heavy subtropical rains rapidly eroded the slopes, and raging torrents rushed down the mountain sides to carve deep V-shaped canyons. Much of the metamorphic layer was removed and carried down to form thick sediments east and west of the mountains.

Later came a time of intense volcanism which added immense quantities of lava, basalt, and volcanic debris to the landscape.

About ten million years ago the Southern Sierra began to grow rapidly. Extensive faulting and tilting along the eastern edge gave the mountains an east-west inclination, a dramatically sheer eastern escarpment, and a soaring crest culminating in Mount Whitney, 14,494 feet in the sky.

2

Sporadic movement upward continues into our own day. The most dramatic rise in historic times was during the Lone Pine earthquake of 1872, when in a few moments the eastern front moved upward at least thirteen feet and sideways about twenty. It can happen again at any time.

Very recently in mountain time—only three million years ago—the Great Ice Age moved in to give the Sierra its present striking form. As the climate became colder, in the high places glaciers began to form. They surged down the canyons, gouging them out, broadening their bases. This happened not once but several times, with glaciers alternately advancing and retreating. At its greatest extent the Tuolumne Glacier was sixty miles long, and covered the meadows 2,000 feet deep. The longest glacier in the Sierra has left behind the longest meadow.

When the last Tuolumne Glacier had retreated, the landscape looked much as it does today. The blanket of metamorphic rock had been swept away except on some of the eastern peaks such as Dana and Gibbs, revealing the gleaming granitic core of the range. The river no longer roared down a tight little valley, but meandered placidly across a broad meadow. Around the meadow were horn peaks (Cathedral, Unicorn, and Echo Crest). The ice had never covered their tops, but had clawed deep cirques into their sides, leaving sharp crests above. Other rock massifs like Fairview, Lembert, and Pothole domes had been rounded and burnished by the glacial scouring until they shone.

On the floor of the meadow were "roches moutonnées": rocks plucked and rounded by the glacial tide that washed over them until they hunched forward like grazing sheep. There were slabs of bedrock polished smooth as mirrors, inscribed here and there with "chatter marks" where a glacier pushing a small rock had made repeated crescent-shaped grooves. And along the rim of the basin, and often criss-crossing it, were humped up moraines dumped by the retreating ice.

However, the glaciers we so admire today on Mounts Lyell and Maclure, in Dana Canyon, and on Mount Conness are not remnants of this Great Ice Age. Rather, they are remains of the Little Ice Age which started about seven hundred years ago in the Sierra, and ended about 1800 A.D. Their continued presence shows us that the time of ice is not yet completely finished.

Meanwhile during the last million years nature, not content with ice, created an equally devastating age of fire. Though the Tuolumne Meadows region was spared, east of it Glass Mountain poured out a burning cloud of ash much greater than the 1980 explosion of Mount

3

Saint Helens. Directly east and 3,000 feet below Tioga Pass is the moon-landscape of the Mono Craters. To early travelers it seemed harsh, lonely, and dead. These somber cones began their eruptions about sixty thousand years ago, spewing forth shattering clouds of pumice and dust and molten flows of volcanic glass that created a treasure trove for the Indian tool and armaments industry.

About thirteen hundred years ago the most recent Mono eruption laid down a layer of ash as far west as the Tenaya Lake region. The ash added mineral content to the mountain soil—rich nutrients for the grasses and flowers and the animals which live upon them. And much more recently, in 1890, there was an underwater eruption in Mono Lake.

Much of the above geology is now accounted for by plate tectonic theory, whereby movement and friction between large plates in the earth's crust produce faulting, volcanism, and mountain building.

At first after the ice melted, there would have been a series of shallow lakes strung along the slightly undulating floor of the basin where the Tuolumne Glacier had been. Gradually they filled in, leaving a smooth and level series of meadows.

They are meadows rather than forest largely because of a drainage pattern. Runoff from the surrounding mountains feeds into a kind of high-mountain saucer. Most of the water finds its way into the streams, but so much seeps underground that the trees can't grow, although grasses and flowers thrive. On higher, drier ground a forest of lodgepole pine blankets the morainal slopes which rim the meadows, and sweeps part way up the mountainsides. And above the forests—the peaks.

Thus we have Tuolumne Meadows, ancient and yet new; rugged and yet soft; isolated, and yet a crossroads of the world.

This is their story.

2

THEN THERE WERE INDIANS

It was the Ice Age which brought the first people. Freezing temperatures locked up vast amounts of sea water in continental ice caps, and the level of the oceans was lowered as much as 100 meters. This left a bridge of land some 900 kilometers wide connecting Asia to Alaska. Across it, perhaps thirty thousand years ago, small bands of people began to move from Siberia, probably following game animals that drifted onto the rich tundra lands on the North American continent.

Gradually they migrated southward both along the coast and down an inland ice-free corridor paralleling the Rocky Mountains. They had reached California by about twelve thousand years ago.

Ten thousand years ago, during the last great glaciation, hunters living in the Mono Basin left behind basalt spear points and arrowheads which tell us they were here. In their time this now-desert landscape would have been partially rimmed by glaciers hanging from the high passes, and partially filled with the waters of prehistoric Lake Russell, whose much smaller descendant is modern Mono Lake.

Then the weather warmed, and by 9,600 years ago people were crossing the mountains.

There have been climatic fluctuations which affected the Tuolumne region many times since. When it was warmer and drier than now, water runoff down the mountainsides decreased, the meadows dried, and forests invaded them. Game animals would leave for more open grazing areas, and the Indians would follow.

Then again it grew moister and cooler. More snowmelt and rain saturated the soil, trees were killed off by standing in water, the forest

5

receded and the meadows enlarged. Deer and bighorn sheep came to browse, and there were abundant grass seeds, gooseberries, and other plants humans could eat. Probably hunters occupied the meadows for the entire summer and brought their families with them. We surmise this because we find bedrock mortars near the base of Lembert Dome where Indian women ground nuts and seeds.

The last of these cold cycles ("The Little Ice Age") started in the fourteenth century and reached its height in the eighteenth. In low-lands east and west of the Sierra more moisture made rich grasslands and widespread shallow lakes and marshes abounding with animals, edible plants, and people. But we can guess that some high mountain gathering grounds and hunting areas were lost under snows that never melted all summer long.

The ancient transmontane trade, however, seems never to have died out completely. Middens (prehistoric living sites) both east and west of the crest show that numerous items were being traded back and forth over the Sierra through most of the last ninety-six centuries. Perhaps during colder years (or decades, or even centuries) trade was disrupted. Yet by the middle of the 1800s much of the recent ice had melted back and trading flourished through Tuolumne Meadows along a route which came to be known as the Mono Trail.

Directly west of Tuolumne Meadows in Yosemite Valley and the foothills lived the Miwok, and directly east in the Mono Basin, the Northern Paiute. Although these peoples differed greatly in language and culture, they had trade ties which endured over many generations. Some intermarriage occurred, and ideas such as basket designs were borrowed back and forth.

Although we are not certain of the exact route, it seems that a trail went from Yosemite Valley up Indian Canyon to Crane Flat, where it joined the ancient Mono Trail to Tuolumne Meadows, Mono Pass, and down Bloody Canyon to the east side. On the high bare places the route was sometimes marked by pine boughs. Down in the woods someone might hang a dead skunk to mark the way, or stash cured venison in a tree for the use of anyone who might need it.

Along this route from east to west passed piñon nuts, dried fly pupae from Mono Lake, pandora moth larvae, baskets, rabbit and buffalo robes, salt, tobacco, and most important of all, obsidian from the Mono Craters. From the west came acorns, berries, beads, paint ingre-dients, arrows, baskets, and abalone shell ornaments which had been traded from people along the coast.

Early white explorers were unaware of the magnitude of this trading network, but they encountered hints of it. After an early snow in October of 1833, explorer Joseph Walker and his party floundered across the Sierra from east to west. They veered too far north to discover Tuolumne Meadows, but managed to be the first white men to see Yosemite Valley from the rim. Somewhere near the north rim they met an Indian climbing toward the east. When he saw them, the Indian threw down the heavy burden basket he was carrying and ran away. The starving explorers discovered it was full of acorns, which they promptly ate. Probably they were on the Mono Trail without perceiving it, and the Indian may have been a Mono Paiute trying to get home before the winter should close down.

The Mono Trail was used for countless generations. Even today if you walk sections of the route you may find here and there chips of glittering obsidian where some hunter whiled away the time making arrowheads as he waited for game or when he bivouacked for the night.

In 1869 John Muir was impressed by these trails and remarked, "Along the main ridges and larger branches of the river Indian trails may be traced, but they are not nearly as distinct as one would expect to find them . . . Indians walk softly and hurt the landscape hardly more than the birds and squirrels, and their brush and bark huts last hardly longer than those of wood rats, while their more enduring monuments, except those wrought on the forests by the fires they made to improve their hunting grounds, vanish in a few centuries."*

As late as the 1880s the trade was still continuing. John Baptiste Lembert told Will Colby in 1894 (we'll meet them both later on), "It was a striking sight when Yosemite and Mono Indians met and camped out on the rocky moraines in the middle of the Tuolumne Meadow . . . in the late summer . . . They selected these camp sites in order to be out where the breezes blew strongest, thus to minimize winged pests. Their colored blankets and clothes and teepees made a gala appearance. Here they traded skins and acorns for pine nuts and obsidian. On the large moraine just east of the Soda Springs they used to fashion their arrow heads as evidenced in the earlier days by the quantities of volcanic glass flakes, with an occasional fine point that had been overlooked. Practically all of these have since been removed by collectors."

The "teepees" were probably bark, pole, or canvas shelters, and the "colored blankets and clothes" would have been of western manu-

---

*Muir thought the ghost forests of lodgepole pine were due to Indian burning. It was much later realized that this was damage by the needleminer moth.

facture, not aboriginal. But the camps and the barter—these were after the Indian custom from time immemorial.

The annual meetings in the meadows had ceased well before 1900. Yet long afterwards acorns were being carried over the mountains and down Bloody Canyon. In 1922 Ranger John W. Bingaman's wife Martha was stranded at Tenaya Lake in October and finally rescued by Bridgeport Tom, a local Indian who had been packing acorns across the mountains. Near the Snow Creek ford they met five other Indians with ten pack animals, all laden with acorns.

In the 1920s the Monos still used acorns, but there were few Yosemites left to pack them to a high mountain rendezvous, and they no longer desired obsidian in trade. So the Monos came yearly to Yosemite Valley to harvest their own nuts.

In time this too passed. Some Yosemite Indians still occasionally harvest, process, and eat acorns, but ninety-six centuries of trade across the mountains have ended, and Tuolumne Meadows and Bloody Canyon see no more traffic in this ancient and nutritious natural food.*

Photo courtesy of National Park Service

Modern Yosemite Indian
in traditional dress.

---

*For a modernized method of preparing acorns and using them, see "Eat Acorns," by Elizabeth O'Neill, *Mother Earth News*, #47, Sept./Oct. 1977.

3

THEN CAME THE SOLDIERS

The life of the Indians with its seasonal round of acorn-gathering in Yosemite Valley, summer expeditions to the high country for deer, and trade across the Sierra via the Mono Trail persisted for a number of years after the coming of white explorers and settlers to California. The Indians watched and waited. Farther north, Washo Indians even spied on the Donner Party, were appalled by their cannibalism and afraid to make contact, but left caches of food from time to time for the starving whites to find. So far though, both Yosemite Valley and Tuolumne Meadows remained untouched by westerners.

During the gold rush of 1849 the foothills were filled with miners and their hangers-on. Trouble between them and the Indians soon broke out, culminating in a raid on a trading post and the deaths of several white men. Settlers spoiling for a fight formed the Mariposa Battalion which headed for the mountains to retaliate with Captain John Boling as commander. They entered Yosemite Valley but found the Indian villages deserted. A few Yosemites had earlier surrendered, but the others were nowhere to be found. Continuing the search, in early May members of the battalion reached regions to the south of Yosemite near the Ritter Range and could clearly see the Minarets.

Again entering the valley, Captain Boling captured several Indians. In a skirmish one of the prisoners was shot. Tenaya, the aging chief of the Yosemites, came upon the body and revealed that it was his own son. Overcome with grief and anger, he harangued the soldiers, telling them to kill him too, but adding that his dead spirit would take revenge.

Instead they kept him under guard while they continued scouring the country for his people. Several forays to the high country were made, one to the top of Yosemite Falls, and one as far as the base of Mount Hoffmann. Finally Captain Boling, with several men and Chief Tenaya, pursued them to the shores of a high mountain lake where they had made a little village. There he captured them all.

In a magnanimous mood the soldiers told the old chief they would name the lake after him. He replied rather tartly that it already had a name: Py-we-ak, "Lake of the Shining Rocks." Very fitting—but it is known today as Lake Tenaya.

That winter Tenaya finally received permission, on a pledge of good behavior, to return to Yosemite, and some of his people slipped away from the reservation to join him. However, the following May (1852) when a party of miners entered the valley, the Indians attacked them and killed two of the miners. The population of nearby Mariposa was aroused, and Lieutenant Tredwell Moore was dispatched with a small company to finish off the Yosemites once and for all.

Moore entered the Little Yosemite on a branch of the Mono Trail and proceeded into the high country where he found a village of twenty-one men, women, and children with white men's articles which he assumed belonged to the dead miners. He ordered the six adult men shot; then, after waiting for reinforcements, pursued Tenaya and a few remnants of the tribe through Tuolumne Meadows—the first white men to enter the meadows, as far as we know. He followed as Tenaya, one step ahead of him, fled to Mono Pass and down Bloody Canyon, and found refuge with the Mono Paiutes on the other side of the Sierra.*

There is a story that the Yosemites and the Monos got into a gambling quarrel, and in the fight that followed, Tenaya was killed. Another version is that the Miwok stole some Mono horses, and the Monos hunted them down and killed Tenaya in retaliation. Still others say that he died a natural death some years later near Savage's Trading Post on the Fresno River. Whenever and wherever he died, the Indians held a great "cry," and Maria Lebrado, his granddaughter, fasted and wailed for three days, as was customary.

The passing of Chief Tenaya ended the era of Indian wars in the Yosemite region and led to the first white penetration of Tuolumne Meadows.

---

*Details in this paragraph which differ from Bunnell derive from a series of letters by Moore recently discovered and shortly to be published in *Mono Basin in the Nineteenth Century* by Thomas C. Fletcher (in press, Genny Smith Books, Palo Alto, CA).

Lake Tenaya.

4

AND MINERS

When Lieutenant Moore was chasing Chief Tenaya over Mono Pass in 1852, he kept one eye cocked for minerals. After exploring the region north and south of Bloody Canyon, he came back to the Soda Springs in Tuolumne Meadows in August, and then returned over the old Mono Trail and back to Mariposa. He returned without the chief, but with some samples of gold.

These caused a great stir in Mariposa. Leroy Vining saw the samples and that same year headed for the mountains with pickaxe at the ready. He brought a company of prospectors who combed the deposits immediately east of Tuolumne Meadows. Doubtless he visited the meadows as well. But Vining was more interested in homesteading than in gold. He built a sawmill and settled down in the canyon which now bears his name at the foot of Tioga Pass. His fellow-prospectors found nothing worth digging for, and dispersed.

Moore's report had also interested James M. Hutchings, the irrepressible promoter of tourism to Yosemite Valley. He publicized the gold rumors, and this stimulated both miners and tourists. Among them, Tom McGee blazed and cleared a horse trail from Big Oak Flat, past Tenaya Lake and through Tuolumne Meadows to Bloody Canyon—approximately the route of the old Mono Trail, and also of the later Tioga Road.

Although it was no highway, by the summer of 1857 many of the miners from the Tuolumne Mines in the foothills struggled over the trail and through Tuolumne Meadows to the Dogtown and Monoville settlements near Mono Lake. Tourism, too, was on its way. In the

Dana City Mine Cabin.

summer of 1858, a party which included a baby in arms came up from Mono Lake en route to Yosemite Valley for a visit.

Mining finally had its day. Early in 1860 a justice of the peace, an ex-sea-captain, a surveyor, a dentist, and a professor set out to prospect the Tioga and Bloody Canyon area. This unlikely party found no gold. However, the dentist, "Doc Chase," had a hunch there was silver on Tioga Hill, back of Gaylor Peak not far from Tioga Pass. In fact, he thought there was "the biggest silver ledge ever discovered," and scratched out a claim notice on a flattened tin can which he planted on the hill. Then he went off to the Aurora gold strike at Monoville and never got back to Tioga again.

Some years went by, and a legend of a lost mine was bruited about. By 1875, the gold and silver mining waltz was somewhat played out, but the echoes lingered on. One day on Tioga Hill a young shepherd named William Brusky found the old flattened tin can dated 1860, and a rusty pick and shovel. Dreaming of riches, he took some ore samples to his father, only to be told they were worthless.

The next summer Brusky dug deeper and found better-looking ore. In 1877, an assay showed it to be "thundering rich" in silver.

News spread rapidly, and prospectors rushed to the scene. By the following year activity in the Tioga Mining District was in full swing. The district extended from the foot of Bloody Canyon, over Mono Pass and down the Dana Fork of the Tuolumne River to Soda Springs, and about eight miles north and south along the crest. At one time there were 350 locations in the district.

A ledge known as the Great Sierra was found parallel to Brusky's old claim, the Sheepherder Lode. Many small claims were shortly combined as the Great Sierra Consolidated Silver Company. Eight million dollars' worth of shares were signed for. In 1882 the town of Bennett-ville was built. It had a brief, gaudy existence with a post office, "ladies," a Chinese cook, and even one glorious shoot-out!

A tunnel was driven into the mountain. The theory was that the tunnel would strike the two lodes at right angles. Meanwhile, men at Dana City over the hill sank a vertical shaft which was to meet the tunnel.

Hauling equipment to this high remote valley was grueling work. Winter brought avalanches and loneliness. Miners fought the bitter cold with firewood and whisky. All the men suffered; a few men died.

In 1883, with Chinese labor, the company built the Tioga Road along McGee's blazed horse trail on the old Mono Trail.

Several fortunes had been invested. But by the summer of 1884, after having driven the tunnel almost eighteen hundred feet into the mountain, and having run out of money without reaching the lode, the managers suspended work. The machinery was abandoned, and the miners melted away like winter snows.

All this furor had little effect on Tuolumne Meadows. The miners could care less about its placid beauty. Yet the sheer number of passers-by on the new road must have had some impact. And the by-now massive occupation of mountain pastures by sheep would have been stimulated for a few seasons by this close-at-hand market for mutton on the hoof.

Many of the mining camps have disappeared without a trace. But in Bennettville the old pine assay office and a barnlike bunkhouse still stand, weathered golden brown by the mountain sun. Dana City above Gaylor Lakes is now a single monumental stone cabin and a row of low stone hovels against the sky. At the head of Bloody Canyon by Mono Pass, a group of crude log structures recalls the Golden Crown Mine, which, it was supposed, would become rich and famous. And here and there—on the flanks of Dana and Gibbs, Kuna Peak and White Mountain—an old foundation, some weathered boards, cabins falling in ruins, and ancient high stumps sawed when the snow was deep—all speak of the ephemeral hectic days of the Tioga Mining District.

5

GEOLOGISTS: THE WHITNEY SURVEY

In the meantime the State of California Geological Survey had come and gone, and left its record of the meadows.

By the end of the 1850s the first most virulent outbreaks of mining fever had subsided, but the new Californians were far from cured. The legislature now reasoned that a team of geologists should be able to indicate exactly where the wealth lay. With a solid scientific basis, land and mining speculation could boom.

The legislature passed an act setting up a state geological survey, to be headed by Josiah Dwight Whitney, one of the top men in the field. He had already taken part in various state surveys, and had published a widely read book, *The Metallic Wealth of the United States.* He considered that minerals were only part of the job, and set out to learn and record *everything* about the geology of California.

A picture of life on the survey comes from Whitney's right-hand man, William H. Brewer. Brewer had grown up on a New York farm, attended Yale, taught agriculture, and studied and traveled in Europe. At the time of Whitney's offer of a job he was thirty-two years old, and his wife and child had recently died. He was disconsolate and needed a change.

He was the official botanist of the expedition, and a number of familiar High Sierra plants carry his name, like Brewer's paintbrush, cinquefoil, lupine, rock cress, and locoweed. Yet plant collecting was the least of his duties. Most of the time he led the field party while Whitney held down the office in San Francisco and made brief visits to his crew.

Brewer was energetic and practical. He busied himself mending wheels and clothes, hiring and firing cooks and helpers, even negotiating loans when they ran short of money due to political chicanery. He led climbs up and down innumerable peaks and on off days took long hikes and mule rides exploring the country. He also managed to be wined and dined by the local gentry and visited ruined missions and Catholic churches, booming mines and sheep camps. After everyone else was in bed at night, he wrote his notebooks and letters to his brother. The letters, having made the rounds of his family, were saved and much later published as *Up and Down California in 1860-1864.*

By June of 1863 when the surveyors reached Yosemite Valley, they were well seasoned to camp life. They clambered to the top of Yosemite Falls and were dazzled by the sea of peaks around them. In a burst of enthusiasm Brewer wrote, "I have seen some of the finest scenery of Switzerland, the Tyrol, and the Bavarian Alps, but I never saw any grander than this."

Along the Mono Trail on the way to Tuolumne Meadows, they climbed and named Mount Hoffmann for the survey's cartographer, Charles F. Hoffmann. Hoffmann was Brewer's most frequent climbing companion and his closest friend on the survey. He was a German trained in Europe, who finally married and settled in the United States. In later years Hoffmann was to become the founding father of American cartography.

By June 26, 1863 they had reached the Soda Springs. In fact, it was they who named the meadows.* Brewer now wrote: "The river valley here forms a flat nearly a mile wide, green and grassy, while around is the grandest alpine scenery. It is a most lovely spot. Several mineral springs are here ... The waters ... are highly tonic, pleasant to the taste, and would be worth a fortune anywhere in the old states."

But they had work to do, and the next day they moved up to the base of the as-yet-unnamed Mount Gibbs. Early the following morning Brewer and Hoffmann scrambled up the snowy slopes of Mount Dana. They spent over four hours on the summit, taking bearings and barometrical readings. Brewer found that "all north, west, and south

---

*In the lowlands, the Tuolumne River had borne this name since 1806 when Padre Muñoz called it after a local tribe, the Taulámne or Tahualamne, possibly Miwok but more probably Yokut who lived in the San Joaquin Valley. Its meaning is unknown.

was a scene of the wildest mountain desolation. On the east, at our feet, lay Mono Lake, an inland sea surrounded by deserts ... It is not often that a man has the opportunity of attaining that height, or of beholding such a scene."

Whitney had not felt up to the climb, but Brewer and Hoffmann were so excited by it that he now decided to try. So the next day Brewer climbed Dana again, this time with Whitney. He reported that Whitney "thought the view the grandest he had ever beheld, although he has seen nearly the whole of Europe."

Early explorers in the west who had cut their teeth on European scenery often strove to make comparisons like this. Our serrated range, drier, glaciated but no longer rich in living glaciers, differs greatly from the dramatic peaks of the Alps, but has an unrivaled radiance of its own.

Brewer noted that they were camped on a "trail that crosses the mountains, over which supplies are packed on mules during the summer to Esmeralda* ... Trains of animals thus pass nearly every week." Tuolumne Meadows was by then something of a highway.

On July 1 Hoffmann and Brewer loaded their gear on a mule and headed up the Lyell Fork of the Tuolumne River to camp at what is now Upper Lyell Base Camp. They were awed by the heavy frost, the wild grandeur of the scene, their loneliness—and the size of the mosquitoes "with twice the ferocity of a southern Secessionist."

The next day they set out to climb the highest and most challenging peak which soared above them. After over seven hours of hard climbing they came to the last pinnacle rising to the summit, and judged it inaccessible. As Francis P. Farquhar remarks, "It seems to us today incredible that two able-bodied men after reaching a point within a few hundred feet of the summit should fail to complete the climb of Mount Lyell. In the history of mountaineering, however, the *appearance* of difficulty in a novel situation has again and again brought about defeat. In this case the explanation seems to be that, in addition to the unaccustomed effects of altitude, the men were tired from slogging through the soft snow and things looked worse than they really were. Since their day hundreds of climbers, many of them quite inexperienced, have made the ascent."

They stopped, took barometric readings, and gave the peak a name. "As we had named the other mountain Mount Dana, after the most

---

*One of the ephemeral mining camps on the east side of the Sierra.

eminent of *American* geologists, we named this Mount Lyell, after the most eminent of *English* geologists."

Always the diplomat, Brewer had straddled the fence in a great scientific controversy of the day. Lyell was the outstanding proponent of the theory that geological processes had operated at a uniform rate for tremendous periods of time to produce the earth's landscape—while Dana held a traditional view that the history of the earth is reckoned in biblical terms, and natural features like mountains and valleys could be explained by sudden cataclysms of short duration. Lyell's view has been borne out by subsequent geologists, and his is the highest mountain. Dana is mostly forgotten. Yet he too has a fine mountain, and a much more accessible one.

After returning from Lyell they celebrated a patriotic Fourth of July at the Soda Springs with a feast of preserved chicken and a huge bonfire. Brewer, a Yankee, was alternately worried and elated by Civil War news, which came through only now and then.

From wandering around Tuolumne Meadows and climbing some of the domes, Brewer wrote, "A great glacier once formed far back in the mountains and passed down the valley, polishing and grooving the rocks for more than a thousand feet up on each side, rounding the granite hills into domes. It must have been as grand in its day as any that are now in Switzerland. But the climate has changed, and it has entirely passed away. There is now no glacier in this state—the climatic conditions do not exist under which any could be formed."

Strange! They had tramped up a sizable glacier on Mount Lyell without suspecting its presence! It was covered by snow. The Lyell Glacier, moreover, occupies a broad, gently sloping field without icefalls and seracs like those Brewer had seen in the Alps. However, years ahead of Muir he had correctly surmised the glacial past of the region.

Two days later they climbed Ragged Peak north of their Soda Springs camp, amid swarms of mosquitoes—the bane of all July visitors to the high country. The next day they took the Mono Trail to Mono Pass and down Bloody Canyon. He proclaimed it "a terrible trail . . . pack trains come down, but the bones of several horses or mules and the stench of another told me that all had not passed safely . . . part of the way the rocks are literally sprinkled with blood from the animals."

He and Hoffmann climbed the Mono Craters, but Brewer was not charmed. He thought the view "desolate enough—barren volcanic mountains standing in a desert cannot form a cheering picture. Lake Mono, that American 'Dead Sea,' lies at the foot." Most people of his time would have agreed; it would take another two or three generations of writers as dissimilar as Mary Austin and Zane Grey to sensitize us to the beauty of the desert.

With his typical openness to new experience, Brewer sampled the ko-chah-bee (dried fly larvae) of Mono Lake. "It does not taste bad," he assured his reader, "and if one were ignorant of its origin, it would make fine soup. Bulls, ducks, snipe, frogs, and Indians fatten on it."

Then they left this region to pursue their explorations elsewhere. Eventually returning to San Francisco on the Sacramento River boat, they met Clarence King, who promptly joined the survey with his friend, James T. Gardiner. King was a brilliant, ambitious charmer, had studied geology at Yale, and after a stint with the Whitney Survey would go on to become the first head of the United States Geological Survey, which he organized from scratch. But the fatal vision of El Dorado seduced him into deserting science and literature for one losing mining venture after another. He was all but forgotten until his classic tale of high adventure, *Mountaineering in the Sierra Nevada*, was resurrected from oblivion and republished in 1935—to the delectation of modern Sierrans.

In 1864 the survey visited the Southern Sierra, where they named Mounts Brewer, Gardiner, and Clarence King. The name of Whitney, who did the least climbing, was given to the highest mountain of all. They returned north with Brewer thirty pounds lighter and Hoffmann so ill he had to be carried. As Hoffmann was resting at Wawona (then Clark's Ranch), Brewer returned one more time to Tuolumne Meadows. This time he accompanied Frederick Law Olmsted and his son John. Olmsted was the famous landscape architect who would later design New York's Central Park, and who is now memorialized at Olmsted Point, one of the finest outlooks along the new Tioga Road.

Brewer and the Olmsteds rode to Tuolumne Meadows and then on to camp near Mono Pass. The culmination was a first ascent of a huge rusty mountain by the pass. John and William walked, but Frederick, who was lame, rode a horse. They named the mountain Gibbs for Harvard professor Wolcott Gibbs, the foremost chemist in the country at the time, who anticipated the discovery of the periodic table. As they lingered on top they noticed a party on the summit of Mount Dana, and the next day they met them at Soda Springs: genuine early-day tourists, including a man in his sixties and a little girl of six. Pioneer days were ending, and Tuolumne Meadows was becoming the center for High Sierra excursions that it has been ever since.

However, funding for the survey had dried up. Critics claimed its work was too grandiose, impractical, and expensive. The legislators had only wanted a quick fix on mineral wealth and valuable land. They declared loudly that science was none of the government's business. Salaries for the survey members were months in arrears, and Brewer started looking for other employment.

In September, 1864 he learned of his appointment to a professorship at Yale. In mid-November he sailed from Oakland for New York by way of Nicaragua, as he had come. He reckoned up his travels in California: 7,564 miles on horseback, 3,101 miles on foot, and 4,440 miles by public conveyance, "Surely a long trail!"

Brewer never came back to California, but spent the rest of his days as a greatly-respected professor of agriculture, receiving many honors. He married again and raised a family. Yet we cannot help suspecting that the most exciting days of his life were in California, and of these, some of the finest were in the High Sierra around Tuolumne Meadows.

Photo courtesy of National Park Service

Survey party in the Yosemite high country in 1867. Brewer is at the right.
The original of this photo, which was taken by Harris, is owned
by Francis P. Farquhar.

21

6

JOHN MUIR ARRIVES

Indians had come to the meadows for trade and hunting. Soldiers, for conquest. Miners, for wealth. And the Whitney Survey, for scientific knowledge. Now something different occurred. John Muir came, not to subdue or exploit, but to glory in a higher beauty and truth.

When in 1869 a sympathetic Irishman named John Delaney hired Muir to take a flock of sheep to the High Sierra, he was setting in motion a chain of events with endless consequences for the meadows and for the American wilderness.

Perhaps it would all have happened anyway. The stage was set, a stage of meadows and glorious mountains. The leading character waited impatiently in the wings. By hook or by crook he *would* get there! Delaney gave him a shepherd's crook and he came.

At thirty, Muir had the strength and skill of a man, the open heart of a boy. After a grueling childhood on a Wisconsin farm he had burst upon the world—or rather, the University of Wisconsin—full of energy and promise. He was an avid student of science, an ingenious amateur inventor, and a shy but engaging companion who won the affection of his professors. Yet the academic life could not hold him. After a couple of years he wandered off to work at harvesting, to become a skilled mechanic, to drift about the continent as far as Florida, Cuba, and Canada, looking, seeking.

By 1868 the search brought him to California and a long walk across the April richness of the Central Valley to Yosemite. There he spent a short enchanted period of mad dashes up waterfalls, and awe-struck hours gazing at the cliffs and meadows and flowers. Then back to work for a winter at odd jobs while he incubated his passion to see the high country.

Enter Delaney. And in early June, 1869, Muir was off on his first journey toward Tuolumne Meadows—along with a shepherd and some two thousand sheep. Delaney seems to have sensed Muir's need, for their agreement was that Muir would oversee the shepherd, but have most of the time free to explore and enjoy the mountains.

Enjoy the mountains—hardly an adequate description! Muir wandered, observed, sketched, and recorded in his journal the peculiarly intense progress of his spiritual journey. The updraft of the mountain air caught him like thistledown and he went spinning breathless, ecstatic across the Sierra.

What in his dour Scottish background or his grinding boyhood had prepared him for this moment? The God of Beauty whom he sees working everywhere seems only distantly related to the Calvinist deity of his youth. The mystery is like that of the meadows and mountains themselves, with their emergent holiness that transcends the separate elements of water and stone and sky.

Immersed as he was in the grandeur about him, Muir still had time to record the less-than-sublime details of sheepherding life. How the shepherd slept in a nest of decaying wood, close enough to the sheep corral to breathe "ammoniacal snuff" all night. How this same shepherd fried his mutton and popped it into a cloth ditty-bag on his belt, to drip grease all day long down his one pair of pants. How the "poor dumb sheep" balked at stream crossings, panicked at bears. And above all, how they gobbled the flowers and despoiled the meadows.

The flock made slow progress upwards, not reaching Tenaya Lake until August 9. Muir dashed ahead over the divide between the Merced and Tuolumne basins, and down to the "flowery lawns" of Tuolumne Meadows. "Here the mountains seem to have been cleared away or set back," he wrote, "so that wide-open views may be had in every direction . . . This is the most spacious and delightful high pleasure-ground I have yet seen. The air is keen and bracing, yet warm during the day; and though lying high in the sky, the surrounding mountains are so much higher, one feels protected as if in a grand hall."

On August 10 they camped near the Soda Springs. A couple of days later they moved the sheep to a "glacier meadow" north of Tuolumne Meadows. It is difficult to be sure exactly which meadow this was, as the forested slopes between Tuolumne Meadows and Mount Conness are banded with a whole series of meadows, each as flowery as the one

Muir describes. Perhaps they chose one of these in preference to the much larger Tuolumne Meadows because it was entirely enclosed in rather dense forest which would form a natural corral for the sheep.

For almost a month the flock remained in this meadow. Rather shortly, Mr. Delaney and the shepherd got into a row and the shepherd left. Mr. Delaney had to go find another one, and for a few days Muir was in command of the sheep. When Delaney returned, Muir was again free to ramble, and he used the rest of the summer to explore the Tuolumne High Country. Descending to the rim of Yosemite Valley, he climbed the Three Brothers for a view. On his return he visited a pair of Portuguese shepherds tormented and terrified by nightly bear raids on their sheep corral.

On August 21 he made a "fine wild excursion" up the old Mono Trail to Mono Pass, down Bloody Canyon to Mono Lake, and back again. As he headed for the pass, "I had to stop many times to examine the shining rocks over which the ancient glacier had passed with tremendous pressure, polishing them so well that they reflected the sunlight like glass in some places." He noticed the sod "full of blue gentians and daisies, kalmia and dwarf vaccinium, calling for recognition as old friends."

"I watched the gradual dwarfing of the pines as I ascended, and the corresponding dwarfing of nearly all the rest of the vegetation. On the slopes of Mammoth Mountain, to the south of the pass,* I saw many gaps in the woods reaching from the upper edges of the timber-line down to the level meadows, where avalanches of snow had descended, sweeping away every tree in their paths as well as the soil they were growing in, leaving the bed-rock bare." These were years of heavy winter; nowadays the avalanche scars are again mostly clothed in thick woods.

As he enters the canyon he notices some Mono Indians approaching him on their way to Yosemite for a load of acorns: dispossessed lords of the mountains shuffling by on their ancient trail.

The pass itself awed and excited him. At night, camped by Summit Lake, he listened to the rising wind while his fire "squirmed and struggled as if ill at ease." Suddenly the full moon rose over the cliff wall. "She seemed to be just on the rim of Bloody Canyon and looking only at me. This was indeed getting near to Nature ... I might say I never before had seen the moon."

---

*This is now called Mammoth Peak (distinguished from Mammoth Mountain near Mammoth Lakes) and is actually to the *west* of Mono Pass.

John Muir, 1907.

Down in the desert Muir sketched Mono Lake, then full to its salty brim and surrounded by a luxuriant desert flora. Far ahead in the future was the capture of its feeder streams by the Los Angeles Department of Water and Power, and the inexorable lowering of lake level, leaving salt-crusted alkali flats open to the scouring desert winds, and threatening myriads of migratory birds with a loss of their feeding grounds, and thousands of California gulls with the loss of their rookery. After this expedition, Muir returned to Tuolumne Meadows.

Much of that summer was spent in studying the landscape. He wrote, "The lakes and meadows are located just where the ancient glaciers bore heaviest at the foot of the steepest parts of their channels." From the summit of Mount Dana he could clearly trace the courses of the Dana and Lyell glaciers as they flowed majestically out of the mountains, met in a vast confluence, and carved the great trough of the Tuolumne Glacier. He saw the sloping moraines on the valley's sides clothed in forests of lodgepole pine, and above them the jagged ring of peaks which had never been covered by ice.

As he read the great dramatic scroll of the landscape he saw the meadows as a green sea of grass rimmed by white bosses of granite. But this was only one of their many enchanting moods. Season after season, then as now, when the first snows melt the land is brown and sere. After a heavy winter much of the meadows may be flooded with a shallow ephemeral lake of serene reflections, the world in double vision, half of it upside down.

As the pools dry or flow back into the river, the parade of the flowers begins. One of the earliest is the aprica saxifrage rising all of two inches on its single red stem, a tiny cream and rusty ball of blossom. With it come the shooting stars, and soon afterwards pussy-toes, bowed heads of faint white which in another week all stand erect. Steer's head and wild garlic, wallflower and senecio soon dot the verdant meadows.

One morning the first Lemmon's paintbrush appears, and by July its pink-purple blossoms will wash the entire expanse with patches of color echoed by elephant heads. By then the grasses and sedges will be drying burnt gold, and in the bare ground between them are pussy-paws, gray and rosy clusters laid on the ground about a central axis like spokes of a wheel.

Late summer. It's back to brown again, but there are still plenty of flowers: Lyall's lupine, alpine goldenrod, white perideridia, lavender meadow aster.

As autumn comes, and comes early, the willows turn gold and flowers thin out. Gooseberries are red and ripe, and blue gentians sprinkle the grasses among waving Sierra asters.

Suddenly the first snow turns the world pewter. Although it melts

Cathedral Peak from near Upper Cathedral Lake, September 1967.

off, we know it's the beginning of the end. For here in the meadows every spring is a rebirth, every autumn a death. Yet just before winter, meadow asters still show their pink eyelashes and yellow eyes, and on October days one still finds Newberry's gentian, steely white like the coming season.

If autumn is a death, winter is a resurrection. The straw-pale meadows are covered with snow, the passes are closed, and the only humans here are winter rangers-in-residence and their visitors, cross-country skiers who slog into paradise during the short, crisp, brilliant, silent days.

It was not given to John Muir to know all these seasons in Tuolumne Meadows. Summer was hastening to its close, and soon the sheep must be taken to lower pastures.

On the twenty-sixth of August there was a strange reddish glow over Mount Dana at dawn. He spent the day contemplating the changing light, the interplay of sun and shade among the few clouds. In a celebrated passage he gave the Sierra its second name. "Probably more free sunshine falls on this majestic range than on any other in the world I've ever seen or heard of. It has the brightest weather, brightest glacier-polished rocks, the greatest abundance of irised spray from its glorious waterfalls, the brightest forest of silver firs and silver pines, more star-shine, moonshine, and perhaps more crystal-shine than any other mountain chain, and its countless mirror lakes, having more light poured into them, glow and spangle most. And how glorious the shining after the short summer showers and after frosty nights when the morning sunbeams are pouring through the crystals on the grass and pine needles, and how ineffably spiritually fine is the morning-glow on the mountain tops and the alpenglow of evening. Well may the Sierra be named, not the Snowy Range, but the Range of Light."

In the time left he made a daring first ascent of soaring Cathedral Peak, and climbed "three of the most commanding of the mountains" around the highest sources of the Tuolumne and Merced rivers. He scoured the landscape for information about glacial erosion and the influence of cleavage joints.

Then on September ninth the flock headed out of the meadows.

Thus ended John Muir's first summer in the high country. In this brief time he had sealed a covenant which he would keep until the end of his life. He would come again. He would never stay so long. But Tuolumne Meadows—and the Sierra—had found their prophet.

7

JOSEPH LE CONTE
AND THE UNIVERSITY EXCURSION PARTY

On July 21, 1870, "saluted by cheers from manly throats, and hand-kerchief-waving by the white hands of women," a group of college students and their forty-six-year-old geology professor rode out of Oakland "at a sweeping trot" and headed for the High Sierra.

The professor, Joseph Le Conte, felt some misgivings. He was a tenderfoot not long out of the south, and had not ridden a horse for ten years. Also, the style of the trip was rougher and harder than he was used to. They would actually cook their own food, wash their own clothes, and sleep on the ground! Still, he longed to see the high country and study its mountains, and when nine of his students proposed the trip, he decided to join them.

They were in high spirits that July morning. Somebody's horse bucked him off, and another horse ran away and had to be chased—all the occasion of rib-splitting hilarity, and rolling on the ground with laughter.

Crossing the hot and dusty Central Valley depressed their spirits. When they stopped at a ranch, one of the men lassoed and made off with some chickens and a turkey. Later when they were cooked and served up, Le Conte pulled a long face and refused to eat stolen goods, although the aroma of roast fowl tormented him.

In the foothills, a local dog or human snitched all of their bacon and cheese. But some young women from a nearby hotel came down to their camp and joined in songs around the camp fire. Le Conte records that one of the boys, Soulé, was "struck" with a plump girl in short bloomers and ribbons whom the party nicknamed Miss Bloomer.

They stopped off to see the Mariposa Grove of Big Trees. Then, singing and yelling and cracking jokes, on to Sentinel Dome for their first panoramic view of the high country, and their first glimpse of Yosemite Valley. They were appropriately overcome. "From that moment," Soulé wrote later, "the study of Yosemite was a lifelong and absorbing interest and delight" to Le Conte (as it was for Soulé himself).

In the valley they reveled in scenery, plunges into the river, dinners out at the hotel, and they met John Muir. Le Conte was deeply impressed with his scientific knowledge and his earnestness. "A man of so much intelligence tending a sawmill!" he exclaimed. "This is California!"

Muir promised to accompany them to Tuolumne Meadows, and on August 8 Soulé exchanged photographs with Miss Bloomer—who had by now also reached Yosemite—and they started for the high country.

In the red fir belt (they called it spruce) they came to a shepherd's camp. No one was about, but strips of mutton hung drying and a pot of mutton stew simmered in the hot ashes. Muir assured his friends that the shepherd would be flattered rather than otherwise if they were to eat the stew, and they fell to. "While we were yet wiping our mustaches ... the shepherd appeared, and was highly amused and pleased at our extravagant praises of his stew." Still hungry, they bought a sheep and butchered it for their noonday dinner, along with bread baked in tilted frying pans before the fire. While cooking in a high wind, Le Conte singed his whiskers and mustache and badly burned his hand with hot bacon fat.

When they reached Lake Tenaya, Le Conte and Muir spent a silent after-dinner hour sitting on a high rock that jutted into the lake and watched the surface first sparkling, then gradually clearing into a perfect mirror of the surrounding mountains. How many of us who came later have spent just such an exquisite hour at that very spot!

Saddling up the next morning, Phelps (the exhibitionist of the party) put on a show by running at his horse, turning a somersault into the air, and landing on the horse's back like an ancient Cretan bull-vaulter.

At last they arrived at Tuolumne Meadows: "A beautiful grassy plain of great extent, thickly enameled with flowers, and surrounded with the most magnificent scenery." Le Conte continues, "Soda Springs is situated on the northern margin of Tuolumne Meadow. It consists of several springs of ice-cold water, bubbling up from the top of a low reddish mound ... It is very pungent, and delightful to the taste. Before dinner we took a swim in the ice-cold water of the Tuolumne River."

Mount Dana beckoned in the distance and they saddled up for an afternoon ride to its base, only to be caught by a tremendous thunderstorm. Throwing all their gear and supplies under some "india-rubber cloths," they piled underneath too and waited out the rain. A debate as to whether to move on or stay at the springs for the night was terminated by Muir and Hawkins when they built a huge camp fire. "With a shout, we ran for fuel, and piled on log after log, until the blaze rose twenty feet high. Before, shivering, crouching, and miserable; now joyous and gloriously happy."

Then the storm ended and meadow and mountain were suffused with golden light. After dinner (more mutton and bread), they hung their blankets around the fire to dry, and Le Conte (ever the professor) gave a lecture on glaciers. Then they rolled up in still-damp blankets on the still-wet ground and slept the sleep of the just.

The next day as they again headed for Mount Dana, they had to wait out another terrific thunderstorm under an overhanging rock. "We are here nearly ten thousand feet above sea level," Le Conte reminds us. "Our appetites are ravenous. We eat up a sheep in a day; a sack (one hundred pounds) of flour lasts us five or six days. Nights are so cool that we are compelled to make huge fires, and sleep near the fire to keep warm."

At that evening's campfire he gave another lecture, this one on the deposits of carbonate springs.

The following day they finally got up Mount Dana. May it comfort us latter-day scramblers up that fine old mountain to know that Le Conte found it "difficult and fatiguing in the extreme." At one point Bolton loosed a large stone, which came barreling down the mountain too fast for Le Conte to jump out of the way, so he opened his legs and it rolled on through and down the mountainside.

Like Brewer, Whitney, and Muir before him, Le Conte was awed. "The view from the top is magnificent beyond description. To the southwest, the sharp, strangely picturesque peaks of the Cathedral group. To the south, in the distance, Mt. Lyell group, with broad patches of snow on their slopes; and near at hand, the bare gray mass of Mt. Gibbs. To the north, the fine outline of Castle Peak,* rising above and dominating the surrounding summits, and to the east, almost at

---

*Now Mount Conness.

our feet, the whole interior valley, including Lake Mono, with its picturesque islands and volcanoes. Stretching away to the west, valleys with grassy meadows and lakes separated by low wooded ridges."

On returning to camp, another storm, another fire. And another lecture, this one on salt and alkaline lakes, in anticipation of what lay ahead. Evening lectures like these would later form part of the early Sierra Club outings.

On August 13 there was frost on the ground. They were off by 6:00 A.M. from what they had named Camp Dana. This seems to have been near the confluence of Parker Pass Creek and the Dana Fork of the Tuolumne River. They followed up Parker Pass Creek to Mono Pass, then down Bloody Canyon, leading their horses to minimize the damage done by the rough trail. As with Muir the previous year, a party of Indians passed, demanding, " 'Give me towaca.' They were evidently incredulous," he continues, "when told that none of the party chewed."

The rest of Le Conte's story passes beyond the Yosemite High Sierra. They lingered briefly to bathe in Mono Lake, but were repelled by the large number of lake flies at the rim, and did not enjoy the slimy feeling of the water. In fact, like Brewer, Le Conte finds it difficult to enjoy the desert. It seems excessively arid and dull to him. And among the rich desert flora he sees only sagebrush. On the other hand, he and Muir climbed one of the craters. Both were fascinated by the volcanic deposits and intrigued by trying to date them. Muir parted from the group in the crater, promising to write Le Conte whenever he noticed any further facts of geological importance.

The party proceeded north to Lake Tahoe and eventually back over the mountains and down to Sacramento, where they boarded a boat for San Francisco and, at 11:30 P.M., another boat to Oakland. Still feisty, the boys raced their horses alongside the train until it left them behind, then galloped through the empty streets of Oakland, "saluted only by barking dogs; dismounted at the stable, bid each other goodnight, and then to our several homes; and our party, our joyous, glorious party, is no more!"

"Alas," ends Le Conte, "how transitory is all earthly joy! Our party is but a type of all earthly life ... full of enjoyment and adventure, but swiftly hastening to be again dissolved and returned to the common fund from which it was drawn. But its memory still lives; its spirit is immortal."

Later Professor Le Conte had his journal printed, with several copies for each member of the party. Thirty years later the Sierra Club reprinted the journal in its entirety in the 1900 issue of the Bulletin. The extra copies were destroyed in the San Francisco earthquake and fire of 1906. The Sierra Club reprinted it in 1930, again in 1950, 1960, and 1971.

So it has, in a sense, become immortal for those who love the High Sierra. An adventure which set no new frontiers, where no avalanches roared, and there was no shooting. A charming Victorian memoir of a long-ago summer in and about Tuolumne Meadows.

Le Conte was a remarkable man, learned in many fields: geology, physics, biology, botany, optics, and anatomy. He would be most famous as a geologist, and as the University of California's most influential teacher in his day. At a time when many felt that evolutionary thought was a threat to traditional religion, he strove to reconcile and synthesize them.

Happily, he would live a long life. He would return many times to the Sierra, and his son after him. But more of that later.

8

THE SHEEPHERDERS' INVASION

We come now to the man everyone in California has heard about, and almost nobody knows. A figure sometimes comic, sometimes romantic, sometimes banal, and even sometimes tragic: the sheepherder.

A note about terminology. Mary Austin, who went about the sheep camps to meet this exotic creature some fifty years ago, is very precise: "The Frenchmen call themselves *bergers*, the Mexicans *boregeros*, the Basques *artzainas*,"* all meaning shepherd, or an owner who travels with the flock. An owner who stays at home is a wool grower, and the sheepherder is "merely a hireling who works the flock in its year-long passage from shearing to shearing."

All this may be, but in California, though we still speak of wool growers, anyone out with the sheep is called a sheepherder, whether he owns them or not.

When Le Conte visited the meadows in 1870 he found the presence of the sheepherders and their large flocks perfectly natural: "The Tuolumne Meadows are celebrated for their fine pasturage. Some twelve to fifteen thousand sheep are now pastured here. They are divided into flocks of about twenty-five hundred to three thousand." Although he was an observant geologist, he seemed unaware of the

---

*The Mexican word should be written *borreguero*, one who tends lambs. The correct Basque term is *artzaiña*, plural *artzaiñak*.

damage done to the meadows by those close-cropping muzzles and sharp hooves. Rather, he took a utilitarian view. "The sheep we bought yesterday is entirely gone—eaten up in one day. We bought another here—a fine, large, fat one. In an hour it was butchered, quartered, and a portion on the fire, cooking."

A fine, fat sheep indeed! The alpine grasses and flowers of the meadows, so fragile, so slow-growing, and so beautiful, were gobbled with sullen delight by the voracious intruders.

Recent intruders they were. Some few domestic sheep had been in California since the 1700s, brought by the Franciscan fathers to the missions. But their numbers were limited, and they left the mountains untouched. The sheep population in the lowlands had peaked in about 1819, then declined as the missions declined. By 1850, there were said to be fewer than twenty thousand sheep in California.

It was the mining madness which brought a veritable sheep invasion. They were chops on the hoof requiring no refrigeration, and furnishing their own transportation to "the diggin's." In 1853 William Hollister drove a flock over the Emigrant Trail from the midwest, and the next year Solomon Jewett shipped a flock by way of Panama. The sheeprush was on.

By the end of the 1850s fine Merino sheep were introduced—extremely hardy and good wool producers. When the Civil War cut off the supply of cotton from the South, the market boomed for wool. Yet now the flocks were being forced from the Central Valley by its fierce dry summers and the preemption of good land for agriculture.

Most of the sheepherders were Basque, with smaller numbers of Portuguese, Scots, and French. They came from lands with ancient pastoral traditions. As long as the populations in their homelands had remained small and the land unlimited, pasturage could be maintained. But as soon as a group outgrew its valley, herds were increased to feed more mouths and the trouble began. Brush was burned off to allow grass to grow; subsequent over-grazing removed groundcover and resulted in erosion; then with a gradual regrowth of new brush, the cycle began again. The well-watered Basque homeland, much like coastal Oregon, can withstand many such depredations. But farther east and south, the wrinkled sere faces of Mediterranean hills show what men and sheep can do to an arid landscape. California, too, is largely an arid land.

Although in Europe most of the immigrant herders had not been professional sheepmen, they knew something of the business. Now in California (as earlier in the South American pampas) they found an opportunity to prosper. Starting as hired sheepherders and saving their wages, they could soon establish herds of their own, rapidly increasing them to enormous flocks which moved about the vast empty landscape. Most herders spoke little or no English, spent long lonely months away from towns and people, and had slight contact with American culture. They dreamed of amassing small fortunes and going home to live out their days—hence they had no motivation to spare the pastures for re-use year after year. And with all that free government pasturage available, the incentive to build up the herds beyond the carrying capacity of the land was very great. So into the California hills they came, devouring and burning as they moved.

Another knowledge the herders brought from the old country: the value of high mountain pastures with their lack of heavy brush and their tender grasses. By the early 1860s the flocks were pouring above the need of fire, to the lush meadows so loved by deer and bighorn—to Tuolumne Meadows, among others, for summer pasture. Near the foot of Mount Dana one can still see a few strange carvings of female figures on the boles of lodgepole pines, where some solitary sheep-herder long ago passed the time with his fantasies. After a season in the High Sierra, they would move down into the foothills again with their fat animals ready for market.

To Muir, the sheepherder's life seemed sordid and degrading. "Coming into his dingy hovel-cabin at night, stupidly weary, he finds nothing to balance and level his life with the universe . . . he just makes a few grimy flapjacks in his unwashed frying-pan, boils a handful of tea, and perhaps fries a few strips of rusty bacon . . . and depends on the genial stupefaction of tobacco for the rest. Then to bed, often without removing the clothing worn during the day."

Mary Austin (who also felt herself outside the pale) gives us the most sympathetic picture of this much-misunderstood character. She says the strange Basque speech led some to conclude they were crazy. And she admits that "the leash of reason does . . . occasionally slip in the big wilderness," as in the case of one Jean who "in a succession of dry years found himself so harassed by settlers and cattlemen occupying his accustomed grounds and defending them with guns and strategies, that he conceived the very earth and sky in league against him, and was found at last roaring about a dry meadow, holding close his starved flock and defying the Powers of the Air." Then she adds, "I hand you up these things as they were told to me . . . [but] with all my seeing into desert places there are three things that of my own knowledge I have not seen—a man who has rediscovered a lost mine, the heirs of one who died of the bite of a sidewinder, and a shepherd who is insane."

Ironically, they were trying to be good shepherds. A good shepherd finds pure water for his flock—though they leave it sullied. He goes far to seek sweet grass—though the roots may be destroyed and the next season barren. He does not understand about soil cover and watersheds. Starting in 1857, the Great Circle route up the east side of the Sierra into the mountains (often through Tuolumne Meadows) and back south again was a great scourge. Grasses and green plants were uprooted and devoured and sagebrush, which the sheep could not destroy, flourished. Trampling hooves prevented water from filtering into the compacted soil, and new grasses could not grow. Then too, as the sheep ate the plants, minerals which had come from the long weathering of rocks and the ancient ash-falls were absorbed into their bodies and carried out of the mountains. This, combined with erosion, left the mountain soils poorer.

It is not clear when Muir became an active foe of the sheepherders. During his first summer in Tuolumne Meadows he had said, "To let sheep trample so divinely fine a place seems barbarous." By the time he visited the Giant Forest in 1875, he called them "hooved locusts," and bitterly opposed their presence. The financial stakes for the sheepherders were high, however, and the High Sierra was, after all, public land. Muir inveighed against them, but he was trying to sweep out the darkness with a very little broom.

In 1876 there was a drought. As waterholes in the lowlands dried up, the impact of sheep on the high mountain meadows increased drastically. Competing for pasturage, the sheepherders began taking potshots at one another. Cattlemen joined the melee, claiming equal rights to despoil the public domain.

By 1890 many trails had been obliterated, streams muddied, and pastures denuded. In those days of horse and mule travel, it became difficult to take pleasure trips to the High Sierra at all—no feed for the animals.

And just when things seemed at their worst, there was to be a turning point. But I am getting ahead of my story.

9

INTERLUDE: SHELLEY DENTON'S CAPER

Who has walked the trails and not met him or his modern-day counterpart? Young, high-spirited, ill-equipped, poorly informed— but he's *doing* it! That was Shelley Wright Denton in 1880 who (while others explored, measured, and climbed) had his own inimitable Sierra adventure in Tuolumne Meadows.

His father, Professor William Denton, had come out to California in 1874 delivering geology lectures up and down the state. While at Mono Lake he had noticed clouds of grebes over the water, thousands of them.

In those days, ladies' hats were fancied up with feathers and even whole stuffed birds. The possibility of a financial killing was not lost on Denton Senior. So six years later his two sons, Shelley and Sherman, with a friend named Bert, set out from New England to make their fortune on Mono Lake grebes.

In early June, 1880 they arrived in Reno, bought a cart for thirty dollars, loaded their heavy trunks full of powder and shot and bird-skinning knives, and headed south. Sometimes they walked, tugging the cart through ruts and dust and mud; when they could find a wagon to haul them, they rode.

They camped for some time at Lee Vining Creek, shooting and skinning birds by the hundreds. But not the thousands, for they had missed the high tide of grebes. So they branched out and slaughtered every possible type of shore and songbird, singing as they worked. As a sideline, they robbed birds' nests, blew out the eggs, and catalogued them in boxes.

They were soon short of funds and began robbing the gulls' nests on Negit Island in Mono Lake for eggs, twenty-five dozen at a time. California gull omelettes soon lost their charm, especially as some eggs were far along in incubation. "Bert wouldn't eat them at first," says Shelley, "but it is all we have." With ten cents they bought "a pound of sugar, four slices of bread, two pieces of meat, and a piece of berry pie."

By June 19 they saw that the grebe jig was up, and decided to hit the Mono Trail for Yosemite Valley. They baked ten loaves of campfire bread and unloaded much of their excess ammunition, but kept one trunk and the cart. With these and fifty-five-pound carpet bags, they toiled up to Moraine Lake near the foot of Bloody Canyon, where they paid a man five dollars to haul most of their stuff to Mono Pass on horses—while *they* dragged the cart.

That night they had wild onions for dinner. "Sherman never eats onions but I should think he liked them from the way he made them disappear." The next day they feasted on twenty-five frogs and six ground squirrels.

It was a hot climb, but all snow at the top. While the temperature dropped to freezing, they built a big fire in the moonlight. Shelley was not immune to scenery and noted, "The effect was grand beyond description."

Their problem was the cart. They had to get up at three in the morning to drag it over the snow before it softened under the hot mountain sun. First they would tow the cart for a distance, then go back to carry up their carpet bags, relay after relay. By noon they reached a deserted sheep corral where they finished off the last of their bacon.

Romance was wearing thin. Shelley tramped around a bit, "but found nothing but snow and woods everywhere. When I got back to camp my feet were wet and cold for my shoes are all coming to pieces. We are all feeling rather blue this evening and hope we shall come to Soda Springs tomorrow where there will be a good road."

They were deceived. The next day (no breakfast) they ran the cart over the snow until they crossed a stream on a snow bridge. It was now sunrise, and they again began relaying their burdens through a long hard day.

Bread for dinner. "I could enjoy this beautiful scenery which is so fine but for the thought that we have nothing to eat but flour or bread and don't know when we shall get out of here or get where there is some more food ... We tried eating the buds on the trees but could not keep them on our stomachs. I would dream at night of eating and would give all I own to have the scraps off the waste heap at home. It got so cold at night my hair would freeze to my boots which I used as a pillow."

The next sunrise they finished their last bread and made it down to Tuolumne Meadows where they faced the Tuolumne River, at that time a roaring torrent seventy-five feet wide and glacier-cold. They now stripped to the buff and waded across, slipping and sliding in the freezing water. But no way could they get their baggage across that rushing river, bankful of snowmelt. Still naked, Sherman walked upstream until he found some logs to cross on.

Just then Sherman sighted a "coon." (Must have been a marmot.) He gave chase, but it slipped down between some big rocks. After shooting it, Sherman saw no way of retrieving it. Finally Shelley squeezed into the crack, seized the bushy tail, and pulled it out.

Carrying this new burden (twelve more pounds), they passed on down the meadows to the bend of the river, where they stopped and cooked their prize. "The meat . . . was very good, anyway it was something to eat."

It was now late afternoon, and no sign of that good road they had been promised. They were getting desperate. Dropping down through the woods they followed a stream which rapidly became larger. Had they taken the wrong route? Was this the beginning of the almost impassable Tuolumne Canyon? The way got steeper, the snow deeper, and the rocks and logs seemed insurmountable. Finally they stumbled on a trail, and at long last concluded that they had too much gear. So, keeping one gun and their valuables, they deserted cart, trunk, birds, eggs, and extra ammunition.

That night, camping by a small stream, Shelley brooded, "We are certainly lost. If I ever get out of these mountains again alive it will be the last time I shall ever go away from civilization."

They were up at sunrise, and had only trudged a short distance when they came to Lake Tenaya and a cabin on the shore. It belonged to John L. Murphy, an old Yosemite guide who had built it during the Tioga mining rush, and took in paying guests in season.

The door was unlocked. Inside they found a treasure trove: flour, beans, ten pounds of bacon, yeast, salt, pepper, sugar, and twelve tins of canned food. Ecstatically they cooked up a six-quart pail of beans, made bread, fried bacon, and spent the day eating. "But I have eaten so much I can hardly walk or sit down and yet I feel hungry. We were nearly starved and now feel really in pain and terribly uncomfortable."

A two-night stand in this outpost of civilization revived them all. On the third day they cleaned up the cabin and left powder and shot with a note saying they had been starving, and were leaving the ammunition to pay for what they had used.

They finally made their way down to Yosemite Valley, "so glad we pulled grass and threw at each other." Shelley continues, "I don't think I shall ever forget this day the first of July 1880. I feel well repaid now for all the work, trouble, suffering, money and time I have spent and shall never regret coming to see the Yosemite Valley."

Even so, they returned one more time to a point near Mount Hoffmann to collect their discarded gear and their precious, battered cart. Before leaving Yosemite they met Mr. Murphy, owner of the Tenaya Lake cabin which they had raided. He said they were welcome to the grub, and wished them godspeed home.

And so, reluctantly, they left the Sierra Nevada and took in the bright lights of San Francisco. Five months later they reached Massachusetts full of tall tales and, like many a mad-eyed goldseeker before and since, with little more than a hole in the pants to show for their adventure.

As for the much-traveled cart, it was bought by a rancher named Mr. Crowell, and in 1931 was still in use on his farm.

Photo courtesy National Park Service. Photographer: Ralph H. Anderson

Mono Lake.

41

Early day visitors at the Soda Springs around a smoky fire. Lembert is third from the right.

10

THE KING OF THE MEADOWS: JOHN LEMBERT AND THE SODA SPRINGS

During these years Tuolumne Meadows was not part of the Yosemite Grant which had become a California State Park. It was simply government land, open to homesteading and sheepherding. Yet only one homesteader ever took root in the meadows.

A fanciful character, quite in tune with the bright romance of the setting, John (or Jean) Baptiste Lembert would become a legend. He hailed from New York State. It's been said he had a classical education, spoke with precision and a certain elegance, and loved books. Yet one picture shows a bearded old fellow riding a mule, the prototype of the the Old Prospector.

Lembert was around and about Yosemite—both valley and high country—for many years. For a while he was winter caretaker of Snow's Hotel in front of Nevada Falls. Perhaps it was then that he learned the habit of solitude. But when the snows grew deep and the silence too loud, he used to walk down to the valley to visit a young woman named Nellie who worked in George Fiske's photographic studio.

Lembert fell quite in love with Nellie, and in his shy and courtly way he begged her to marry him. But she had other prospects in mind and turned him down. Her refusal rankled in his memory the rest of his life.

As far as we know this was his first and last romance. By now a confirmed outsider, he built a cabin among the Indians down the Merced River Canyon below the valley. He did not have the typical Yankee aversion to Indians, and lived quite happily among them, gradually learning their customs. Perhaps he became too interested. There was a falling out when he went digging up their graves looking for shell money and relics. After that he was more of a loner than ever.

Each spring Lembert would move up to Tuolumne Meadows, where he built a cabin at the Soda Springs. The meadows became his world, his domain. Though he lived alone, he welcomed all who came through, and earned the name, "The Friendly Hermit of Tuolumne Meadows."

Many of the sheepherders were his friends, and kept him supplied with mutton and tall tales told by the fire. In fact, after sheepherding became illegal up there, he used to warn them when army rangers approached. He missed these old cronies when they were finally excluded and came no more to his hearth.

He filed a homestead claim in 1885. Yet he felt uneasy about his status as a homesteader. To solidify his claim, he drove a large flock of angora goats up from the lowlands. But one fall he lingered too long, and was caught by an early storm. Abandoning the goats to their fate, Lembert managed to struggle out of the mountains and survive.

After that, he filed a mining claim as another way of ensuring his hold on the property. He sank a shaft among the granite rocks below where Parsons Lodge now stands. It was later filled in, but traces of this fruitless excavation still remain.

What a strange one Lembert was! In 1949 William Colby wrote about him, from his memories of fifty years before. He recalled that Lembert had written long poems about the mountains and their grandeur. In his loneliness the old man constructed an entire mythology, naming the mountains and natural features around him for the characters he invented. On the various sides of Lembert Dome he saw a picture of his own history: from the cabin, the features of a youth showed on the face; on the south side, a middle-aged man; and from the north side, an aged visage with long flowing beard.

He was King of the Meadows, and the woman who had so cruelly rejected him became his queen and ruled with him—until she henpecked him too much and he turned her into a hen-shaped white-bark pine on top of the dome. Pursuing the image, he collected a pile of waterworn stones which he said were the eggs she had laid. An imaginary woman-friend of hers had the temerity to intercede for the poor transmuted queen, and was forthwith turned into stone, the upper part of Cathedral Peak.

Some people thought Lembert was out of his mind, but according to Colby, he knew quite well that these were fantasies.

Lembert Dome seen across the meadows.

One writer claims that Lembert lived at first in the shelter which still stands over the Soda Springs themselves, but this seems unlikely. By the time Colby knew him, he had built a rough one-room cabin approximately where Parsons Lodge is now located. It had a stone foundation, a crude fireplace and chimney, and a lean-to for storing hay for his donkey. It was built of chinked logs and was finished with shakes on the sides and the roof. Colby tells of spending the long summer evenings of 1894 talking with Lembert in the doorway of the cabin.

Lembert put up a log fence around his land to keep out the sheep, and for a fee made it available for grazing by parties coming through with stock. He thought very highly of the soda springs and used to bottle their water for sale in Yosemite Valley where, reported mountain climber George Bayley, "it is the only soda water in use." Lembert may have expected the springs to make him rich by becoming a famous health spa.

That was the heyday of spas, when the well-to-do flocked to mineral springs to "take the waters." The soda springs, with their bubbly tonic-water rich in calcium carbonate and other minerals, seemed a natural. They never made it, but for the last hundred years hikers have paused for a ritual taste which brings either wry faces or smiles of delight. A jot of lemonade powder or a dash of scotch will dress it up, though many prefer it straight: the Perrier of the Sierra.

It was early in the 1890s when a government scientific expedition came through the meadows. Although they considered Lembert a bit touched in the head, they enlisted his help in collecting plants and insects. Upon leaving, they gave him addresses to which he could send specimens for payment. Soon he was earning money by supplying museums all over the world. He claimed that some of his finds were later named for him.

This new activity delighted Lembert. He was already a fair all-round naturalist, and butterflies were his passion. He had all the standard works on the subject, and read avidly anything new that came his way. University students who stopped by the Soda Springs got in the habit of giving him whatever reading matter they had, and would send him books when they got back to the city. He corresponded with lepidopterists in the east, and at his death there was an obituary in the *Entomological News*.

So he lived in his mountain-girt kingdom, spinning stories, hewing wood, and chasing butterflies. For a long time he was the only one who knew where to find the rare, pale-green Behr's Sulphur Butterfly

(*Colias behrii*), which has its center in Tuolumne Meadows. It was part of his rich and secret life.*

Some thought he was almost penniless. But living on little, he managed to save quite a wad. The local storekeeper in the valley once remonstrated with him when he pulled out a roll of bills that may have totaled a thousand dollars, to peel off one or two in payment for some groceries. "You might get robbed," he exclaimed, "carrying all that money around!"

"Oh," Lembert replied, "I'm not worried about my neighbors, and I guess you're all right."

His trust was too great. Every fall he would return to Merced Canyon. And one winter in the late '90s he was found murdered in his cabin there—presumably for his money. The murderers were never apprehended.

So ended the first and last King of Tuolumne Meadows.

Eventually Lembert's property passed into the hands of the Sierra Club. Some time after the transfer, Sierra Club members found a sheaf of Lembert's poems and a little diary buried in an old stump. These were sent to the club headquarters in San Francisco, only to be destroyed (with all other early Sierra Club records) in the San Francisco fire of 1906.

Visitors can still drink soda water in the little springhouse he built about the springs. And looking up to Lembert Dome, perhaps they can see the old man's proud and mournful face gazing down at them.

Behr's Sulphur Butterfly *(Colias Behrii)*

---

*In the 1950s another greenish butterfly of high elevations in the park was discovered and named Lembert's Hair-Streak (*Callophrys lembertii*) in his honor.

11

JOHN MUIR RETURNS AND THE YOSEMITE HIGH COUNTRY BECOMES A NATIONAL PARK

We last left John Muir in 1869 in his first rhapsodic discovery of Tuolumne Meadows. In the same years as the Golden Age of Mountaineering in the Alps, Muir had come into his own Golden Age.

Now the years had rolled by. During the 1870s, while certified geologists pontificated about water erosion and downfaulting cataclysms as the cause of Yosemite Valley, Muir had a different vision: an age of glaciers. Meticulously he hunted up the Yosemite Creek Basin for evidence of a glacier which, he was sure, must have poured over the north wall into the valley. When he found what he was looking for, he was ecstatic. Having traced his quarry to its source on the shoulder of Mount Hoffmann, he mapped out the length and depth of the great departed river of ice. Between trips skyward sleuthing the past, he gradually put together an article, "The Death of a Glacier," which was published by the *New York Tribune* on December 5, 1871.

The weight of scientific authority said there were no glaciers left in the Sierra. But in October of that year came a great moment in the Merced Range when he discovered under morainal debris the freshly ground blue-gray silt that revealed the presence of a living glacier. The following summer he went to Mount Lyell to plant stakes across the Maclure lobe of the Lyell Glacier to measure its flow. Within two years he found no fewer than sixty-five living glaciers in the Sierra.

In 1871 he left the Soda Springs and descended the gorge of the Tuolumne Canyon, which had until then been considered impassable.

In mid-October of 1872 he made a mad solo foray down the crest (without blanket but with his proverbial bag of bread crumbs) and

consummated a thrilling and dangerous first ascent of the north face of
Mount Ritter. His description of this climb is one of the classics of
mountaineering literature. Scaling the sheer sunless cliff, he suddenly
found himself spread-eagled on the rock, unable to move up or down.
His nerves failed and he thought he was lost. "Then," he recounts, "as
if my body, finding the ordinary dominion of mind insufficient,
pushed it aside, I became possessed of a new sense. My quivering
nerves, taken over by my other self, instinct, or guardian angel—call it
what you will, became inflexible. My eyes became preternaturally
clear, and every rift, flaw, niche, and tablet in the cliff ahead, were seen
as through a microscope. At any rate the danger was safely passed, I
scarcely know how, and shortly after noon I leaped with wild freedom,
into the sunlight upon the highest crag of the summit. Had I been
borne aloft upon wings, my deliverance could not have been more
complete."

In 1873 he went down the Tuolumne Canyon again, this time with
Mrs. Jeanne Carr, the botanist Albert Kellogg (for whom Yosemite's
stately black oak is named), and the artist, William Keith.

That same autumn he ventured for the first time into the wildly
scenic areas that are now encompassed in Sequoia and Kings Canyon
national parks. The logging off of the forests and the devastation by
sheep sickened him. He wrote in his journal, "Nine tenths of the
whole surface of the Sierra has been swept away by the scourge. It
demands legislative interference." Then on south down the range. In a
freezing storm he spent a night on the peak now called Mount Muir.
Two days later he climbed Mount Whitney. That winter he prepared
ten superb articles for the *Overland Monthly,* "Studies in the Sierra."
He was now one of their leading contributors.

The following summer (1874) he was in Tuolumne Meadows again.
Having completed his glacial studies, he now wrote, "This Merced
and Tuolumne chapter of my life is done." He was inexorably moving
on to new interests, new mountains, and a more generalized study of
nature.

Now, as more and more people came to accept his theories of
glaciation, they discovered that he offered them something besides: a
gospel of wilderness. "Wildness," he wrote, "is a necessity . . . mountain parks and reservations are useful not only as fountains of timber
and irrigating rivers, but as fountains of life." He had discovered
within himself the courage and the will to be the evangelist of wildness
and, if necessary, its politician. By 1876 he published his first article
urging government control of the forests. He was ahead of his time.

By the time he was forty he came to long for close companionship and a family of his own. The solitary ragged mountaineer with the light in his eye was gradually rejoining the human race. Mrs. Carr introduced him to Louie Strentzel, daughter of a wealthy rancher in Martinez. In 1880 he and Louie were married.

At first he tried to balance the old life with the new. He plunged into management of the ranch, yet also made extensive journeys to Alaska. In the winter of 1881 he worked on the preparation of two bills to be introduced in Congress, proposing the enlargement of the grants protecting both Yosemite Valley and the Mariposa Big Tree Grove, as well as the establishment of a California State Park. Again, he was ahead of his time. Both bills died in committee.

Now John Muir began to withdraw from public life. He wrote little and wandered no more. For eight years—most of the '80s—he remained at his post, developing the ranch into a top grape producer, laying by a lot of money, and enjoying the childhood of his two daughters.

Friends and admirers were dismayed. They required his leadership and inspiration. No one else seemed capable of carrying the torch he had lit.

In time, hard work with no vacations began to tell upon his health. He had the sickness of the lowlands that could only be cured on the heights. By 1888, with a sense of desperation, he was persuaded to go to Mount Rainier for several months. In his absence, his wife decided to sell off and lease out various parts of the huge ranch. Thus he was gradually freed forever from the drudgery that was killing his spirit. At Mount Rainier he rededicated himself to the wilderness.

He was now fifty. Suddenly he found his old passion and began to write with renewed power. One of those who was most relieved was his friend, Robert Underwood Johnson of *Century Magazine*. Johnson had been goading him for years to return to the pen and the trail. Now in June of 1889 they decided to go together to Tuolumne Meadows, "to talk."

First they visited Yosemite Valley. Muir was shocked. Even though it was a state park presumably protected for the use of the people, the whole valley seemed given over to commercialism and exploitation. The former garden spot was full of ugly hotels and fenced-in lots; the elysian meadows plowed up to grow hay for horses.

Then to Tuolumne Meadows, "Muir, as usual, taking the worst of things provided—in this case the most obstinate and lazy piece of horse flesh out of fiction," wrote Johnson.

Photo courtesy of National Park Service. Photographer: Underwood and Underwood

John Muir.

The meadows—Tuolumne Meadows—the holy place where Muir had once, in a sense, been born again! Another rebirth occurred now, a rebirth of sorrow and anger and new dedication.

A quarter century of sheepherding had taken its toll. Lofty trees were charred stumps, flowery lawns were dusty and bare, clear streams were trampled and muddy. With little underbrush left to hold the winter snows, they melted off in early torrents, leaving the waterfalls below dry all summer. Only the peaks remained inviolate. With tears in his voice, Muir began to speak of the havoc man had wrought in one of Nature's most glorious gardens.

History is sometimes made with guns and flags, but this time it was made over a campfire at the Soda Springs, and we are all richer for it. For Johnson had a plan. Let them work together, he and Muir, to make this precious Yosemite high country into a national park. Yellowstone had been saved. Why not Yosemite?

Muir was heart-weary with what he had seen, and had little faith in such a scheme. But Johnson persuaded him to write two articles for the *Century Magazine.* First he would describe the beauties of the region, and then he would propose to the American people to preserve this land for all time as a park. Meanwhile he, Johnson, would pull strings in the east, lining up influential people behind the proposal so that when a bill was introduced in Congress, there would already be a wave of support among the public at large.

The sleeping giant was now awake. When he came down from this fateful journey to the meadows, Muir wrote as eloquently as he ever had. He wrote of beauty, and of the destruction of beauty; of the stripped meadows, the despoiled forests, and the ruined watersheds.

Fortunately for Yosemite, John W. Noble, secretary of the interior under President Harrison, had read Muir's writings and had been converted. Meanwhile, a group in Visalia had been agitating for protection of the Tulare County forests which included large stands of Sequoia gigantea—just then being logged off in indecent haste by private groups.

The impact of these two movements coalesced in the Congress. The previous March (1890) Representative William Vandever from Ventura County had introduced a bill for Sierra forest protection in the House of Representatives (HB 8550). Due to political pressure, it excluded the Giant Forest region in the south, and also proposed a very limited portion of the Yosemite High Sierra for inclusion—omitting most of the Tuolumne River watershed, Tuolumne Meadows, Tenaya Lake, and the Ritter Range.

Johnson was very disappointed, and appeared before the House Committee on Public Lands several times to convince them the bill did not go far enough. Muir wrote, "The Yosemite Reservation ought to include all the Yosemite fountains. They all lie in a compact mass of mountains that are glorious scenery, easily accessible from the grand Yosemite centre, and are not valuable for any other use than the use of beauty."

The Southern Pacific Railroad, then a dominant force in California politics, seems also to have favored the parks. It envisioned transporting tourists to them in great numbers.

Now Muir's articles appeared in *Century Magazine*. He was widely quoted in newspaper interviews and articles. Within a few weeks, the cause of Tuolumne Meadows and of all Sierra forests and meadows had become a nationwide cause. Under this pressure, a second bill (H.R. 12187) was substituted for Vendever's original bill, extending the Yosemite Reservation to include the above vital areas, and quickly amended to include the Giant Forest region. Both Noble and Harrison backed it. There was no time for the customary printing of the bill. On September 30, the last day of the session, it cleared both houses of Congress, and was signed into law by President Harrison on October 1, 1890. The campfire vision in Tuolumne Meadows had become a reality.

With the establishment of Yosemite, Sequoia, and General Grant national parks, much of the finest scenery and the noblest forests of the Sierra would be saved. Not the least of these was Tuolumne Meadows.

Photo courtesy National Park Service

Sheep grazing in high mountain meadow.

12

THE ARMY TO THE RESCUE!

Congress had created Yosemite National Park as a ring around Yosemite Valley, which was still owned by the state. The ring had a vast circumference, much of it precipitous and trailless wilderness, through which sheepmen, cattlemen and poachers could easily penetrate. Unfortunately, Congress had neither provided for an administration, nor appropriated funds for running the park, nor established penalties for its desecration.

There was already a precedent for managing a national park. As in Yellowstone, the government called out the army to defend Yosemite, Sequoia, and General Grant parks. A small body of cavalry, trained to fight, had now willy-nilly to forge themselves into a wilderness patrol for meadows, forests, and wildlife.

They came, they saw, and they did a magnificent job.

Things had come to a dreadful pass. The sheepherders had divided the country up into private domains, and they drove out or killed any herders who trespassed on their territories. Meadows that might have supported 8,000 sheep groaned under the juggernaut of 40,000. Whole watersheds suffered from flooding and subsequent drought because of the trampling of the soil and stripping of the vegetation. "Even of that area which has been sacredly set aside as the Yosemite Reservation," wrote Acting Superintendent Colonel Forsythe, "the threat was openly made by the marauding sheep herders, who have devastated Spain and Portugal, that they would 'burn the Government out.'"

And so in 1891 Captain Abram Epperson Wood of the Fourth Cavalry became the first acting superintendent of Yosemite National Park. He set up his headquarters near the southwestern border of the park, where in the spring herders massed almost a hundred thousand sheep preparatory to invading the high pastures. To their consternation they found the army blocking their way.

Captain Wood realized he was in a bind, for he was trying to enforce a law with no teeth in it. He first tried appealing to the owners. He found the cattlemen fairly cooperative, promising to get rid of the offending stock before the end of the year. The sheepmen, however, appeared intent on their annual migration despite the force of the law. "Where their herds go a desert follows in their wake," wrote Captain Wood.

"I had to adopt some plan of action," he continued, "that would thoroughly frighten the owners as well as the herders, or my men and horses would be worn out by perpetually scouring these almost impassible [sic] mountains, and even then, as soon as our backs were turned the herds would be slipped in and grazed until another patrol came along."

As sheep poured over the border, Captain Wood first sent a man to warn the sheepherders to leave the park. After "a reasonable lapse of time," he had the herders who were trespassing picked up and brought to his headquarters. This scared them. But when they found that they were merely warned and set loose, they soon returned to their old ways.

Now the captain escalated. When his men picked up an invading sheepherder, they took four or five days to march him across the park to another border and set him free. By the time the distraught sheepherder managed to get back to his herds, they had usually been reduced by the attacks of wild animals and scattered. After such an incident the owner was less likely to order his herders to enter the park.

The sheepherders now became very cautious and, knowing the terrain like the back of a hand, they were able to take back country routes to remote sections of the park. They set up a system of scouts who spied from mountaintops and set warning fires when troops were seen approaching. The army patrols could watch these fires precede them as they moved through the mountains, and found threatening notices nailed to trees along the trails.

Park superintendents continually pressed the government to set penalties for trespassing, but their pleas went unheard, whether by design or by neglect.

Captain Wood, meanwhile, became desperately ill with cancer of the tongue, suffering (as Colonel Benson later wrote) "the tortures of the damned." He was unable to continue the struggle with the sheepmen, and died in 1894.

That year First Lieutenant N. F. McClure took twelve mounted men and five mule-loads of provisions to Tuolumne Meadows, where he heard the sheep were thick. By the time he reached the meadows the flocks had escaped up side canyons. He followed and finally arrested four herders and their pack train near Mount Conness. Later in Virginia Canyon he came on two large flocks. The herders scrambled up into the rocks and got away. "So I had one or two shots fired to frighten them," he reported. "I do not think that they have stopped running yet."

In 1895 Captain Rodgers was in charge, followed the next year by Colonel Young. They renewed the struggle. But as late as 1897, hikers in the High Sierra were advised in the Sierra Club Bulletin to take lemons "to disguise the unpleasant flavor of water from meadows where sheep had pastured."

Another serious problem was poaching, and it wasn't until 1896 that any serious effort was made to keep fire-arms out of the park. In a society that was quick on the draw, and that cherished its constitutional right to bear arms, this was the ultimate affront. Even a senator tried to use his official influence to allow his friends to bring their guns into the park. The senator was unsuccessful, for the doughty Colonel Young didn't hesitate to take on Congress itself on behalf of the park he had been sworn to defend.

These defenders of the park were few, but seemed like many. One of them, Major Forsythe, came in 1895 and returned many times, finally, from 1909 through 1912, as acting superintendent.

Then there was Second Lieutenant Harry C. Benson. He was far more than a soldier. He was an outdoorsman of the old school, adept at Indian scouting, tireless in wilderness patrol, and knowledgeable about nature. His specialty was birds.

In Yosemite Benson was in the saddle for days on end, covering all sections of the park—which at that time extended all the way to Devil's Postpile. He discovered that there were a few well-marked trails, mostly made by the mules which brought in supplies once a month to the sheepherders. He blazed these routes while chasing sheep. Soon the sheepherders began muttering down in the lowlands that they would kill him on sight. "They, however, always took care not to be seen by me."

The army followed existing trails wherever possible, but many routes had to be painstakingly worked out without previous guidance. With military thoroughness, the officers began constructing trails. Even today, when you find a large "T" deeply engraved on an old tree along a high country trail, you can be pretty certain it was left there by the army before 1914.

Cavalryman Gabriel Sovulewski in camp, 1896. Sovulewski remained as a ranger after the cavalry left and lived out his life in Yosemite.

The old Indian route from Wawona to Tuolumne Meadows via Cathedral Pass was made into a good trail, as was the route from Tuolumne Meadows to Young Lake. They put in the old high trail up Little Yosemite Valley to Merced Lake, over Vogelsang Pass, and down Rafferty Creek to Tuolumne Meadows, and the present trail from the meadows up Lyell Fork of the Tuolumne to Donohue Pass. (This is named for Sergeant Donohue of the United States Cavalry, who made a first ascent of Donohue Peak in 1895 on horseback.) And they built the trail to the vicinity of Glen Aulin, then up Alkali Creek to Cold, Virginia, and Matterhorn canyons.

To sum up, by 1914 the main features of today's excellent trail system had been laid down, largely by the army.

Benson and his fellows were equally diligent in planting fish. A fish hatchery had been started at Wawona, and the soldiers set out to transport fingerlings to every stream and lake they could reach. At that time there were almost no fish in the park, except in the Merced River in Yosemite Valley, and in the Tuolumne River only as high as Hetch Hetchy. Because of their efforts, we now have fishing in Tuolumne Meadows.

When the Spanish American War broke out in 1898, the troops assigned to Yosemite were withdrawn, and eleven civilians were hired to patrol the park. They continued the army's methods, going mounted and armed. "During the period from June 25th until September 1st (1898) they reported they had expelled from the park 189,000 head of sheep, 350 head of horses, 1,000 head of cattle, and confiscated 27 firearms," recounts Ranger Bingaman.

The troops returned to the park in August of the same year. That September when they went back to San Francisco, funds were made available to appoint Archie Leonard and Charles Ledig, the first official civilian rangers. They remained through the winter, and for many years thereafter.

The army managed the park for twenty-three years, under a series of eighteen commanding officers. Many were outstanding. For all of that time, it was a job that required intensity and devotion. Although long gone from the park, their memory lingers on in place names like Smedberg Lake, Benson Lake, Rodgers Lake, and Rafferty Creek.

13

WILLIAM KEITH PAINTS
THE RANGE OF LIGHT

Life in the meadows was not all sheepmen-and-soldiers or survey-ors-and-peaks. Artists came also, to add their visual images to the words of writers in extolling and protecting the high places. One of these was William Keith.

Born in Scotland in 1838, Keith came to New York as a boy, and later traveled steerage to San Francisco as a young book engraver. There he married Elizabeth Emerson, an artist who drew him to the out of doors for sketching and painting. One of his earliest watercolors was of Yosemite Valley. He came to see that painting was his natural occupation, gave up his job, and opened a studio.

In the lush prosperity of the 1860s there was a good market for art, as many newly-rich San Franciscans embellished their homes with the trappings of culture. Soon Keith had earned enough selling his pic-tures to take his family to Düsseldorf, Germany. Bierstadt, the cele-brated landscape painter, had been trained in Düsseldorf, and Keith wanted some European polish to emulate him. In 1870 the Franco-Prussian War broke out, and the Keiths returned to California.

In the autumn of 1872 while John Muir was working in Yosemite Valley, Keith arrived with two artist friends and a letter of introduction from Muir's friend, Mrs. Carr. The two Scots, Muir and Keith, hit it off immediately and were soon calling each other Willie and Johnnie, and trading ethnic jokes. Their quick intimacy ripened into a lifelong friendship.

Keith was looking for a scene to paint, something which would seem to him more of a picture than the massive undifferentiated Sierra he had seen so far.

"Yes," said Muir, "I saw it only yesterday. The crown of the Sierra is a picture hung on the sky, and mind you, it needs none of your selection or 'composition.' I'll take you there tomorrow."

Muir was delighted to lead them to Tuolumne Meadows. "There's naebody like a Scotchman to see beauty," he said. They rode up the Lyell Fork to the point where they could see the glacier-hung presence of Mount Lyell rising majestically above them. Dismounting, they enjoyed a moment of silent awe, and then Keith dashed forward waving his arms and shouting.

"It was the grandest thing I ever saw," he wrote. "It was late in October . . . The frost had changed the grasses and a kind of willow to the most brilliant yellows and reds, these contrasting with the two leaved pine and Williamson spruce* . . . the cold gray rocks, and the colder snow, made a glorious sight." Keith's fine big painting of this scene now hangs in Saint Mary's College, California, and commemorates his first contact with Muir and with the High Sierra.

It was while the three artists were contentedly painting in Lyell Canyon that Muir left them for his solitary climb of Mount Ritter.

That November Keith and company took Muir back to San Francisco with them. From this time on, the two were like brothers. Keith, who had contact with the richest and most powerful men of the city, introduced Muir to many who could help him. Later they both joined the celebrated Bohemian Club. Keith encouraged Muir in his writing, and when Muir began to publish, he praised Keith's paintings to the skies, and thus brought many lucrative commissions his way. Muir and Keith, along with John Swett, the first state superintendent of schools, spent much time together both winter and summer.

In 1874 Keith, Muir, Kellogg, and Mrs. Carr went down the Tuolumne River Canyon and back, starting and finishing in Tuolumne Meadows. It was an arduous thirteen day trip, sliding, clambering, and crawling over the rocks. Bears broke into their food caches, rattlesnakes terrorized them, and the last three days they were on short rations and half sick from overeating sour wild plums. On the return, Keith went ahead and arrived at the top "delirious with hunger and fatigue" to find the packer who had agreed to meet them with provisions, "and I had a right royal feast of mutton chops and sugar!"

"Immediately after Keith's second outing with Muir," writes Brother Cornelius, his biographer, "we see a remarkable change in his painting. No melodramatic 'stage'-light in the sky, but a very soft

---

*lodgepole pine and mountain hemlock

"Mount Lyell, California Sierra, 1874" by William Keith. The painting is a part of the permanent collection at the art gallery at Saint Mary's College.

grayish tint, faintly suffused with blue, as pure, but paler than the forget-me-not." In fact, Muir gave Keith much advice on his painting, all in the direction of more naturalness. Muir thought so highly of his work—especially as Keith followed his suggestions—that he praised him far and wide. Muir's praise was largely responsible for a rush to buy Keith's pictures, and he became rich and as highly regarded as Bierstadt and Hill.

In 1875 Keith printed an article in the *Overland Monthly* describing a July pack trip with Muir, Swett, and a Mr. McChesney. As they rode out of Yosemite Valley in a rain, Keith was fascinated by the grayish rocks, the wispy clouds and soft foggy effects. On the second day at Tenaya Lake he studied the colors of rock and water and noted the curious gradation from pale yellow-green to midnight blue which characterizes Tenaya. They went on to the Soda Springs, over Mono Pass, down Bloody Canyon to Mono Lake, and back to Mount Ritter.

There were many more such trips. Each time Keith made sketches which he later translated onto large canvases. By 1882 he had danced a Scottish jig on the top of Mount Whitney and explored the length of the Sierra. And then his life, and his painting, changed dramatically. Elizabeth died. Although he continued to do landscapes, they moved away from the epic to the more personal and tender.

In 1883 he married again. His second wife, Mary, was a lawyer and a Bay Area leader in the movement for women's suffrage. Keith supported her efforts.

On a second trip to Europe Keith was influenced by Impressionism. He came to see that it was impossible to get all of nature's grandeur onto a canvas. Rather, it must be suggested, so that the grandeur is recreated in the mind of the viewer. He stopped doing the big all-inclusive canvases, and wrote, "Since I have got to look at Nature in this way . . . Mr. Muir thinks of me as one of the lost, a son of perdition." Still, in spite of their arguments over how to paint a picture, they remained close friends.

Keith's studio in the city became a meeting place for kindred souls like Muir, and it was these meetings which in time evolved into the organization of the Sierra Club, with Keith a charter member. Many of this lively group lived in Berkeley not far from his home, and were in and out of each other's houses for evenings which featured charades, skits, singing, and animated conversation. Keith was a talented and popular singer.

He was generous toward his friends. Often after a Sierra Club trip he would paint scenes from his sketches and give them as gifts to his fellow-hikers. Among others, he painted a portrait of Joseph Le Conte. Many club members bought his paintings. (Saint Mary's College now has a large collection of them.)

In 1903 when President Theodore Roosevelt visited Yosemite with Muir, Keith was invited to go along. He declined. Roosevelt, he declared, was a hunter, and cruelty to animals was a bad example for the country. He was a lifetime member of the Society for the Prevention of Cruelty to Animals.

Keith had a long and prosperous life, surrounded by loving friends and happy in the natural world which he tried to depict and interpret. In his seventies he and Muir were still visiting back and forth. Keith was still painting, and Muir writing. When in 1911 Keith died, Muir mourned him deeply. Shortly afterward John Swett followed, and Muir himself was not far behind.

Keith was acclaimed in his own day as one of America's foremost artists, yet now he has gone out of fashion and is mostly forgotten. Nevertheless, we have still his paintings that reflect the vanished sunshine of his days in the High Sierra.

He is memorialized by a splendid mountain in Center Basin in the Southern Sierra, which was named Mount Keith by a Sierra Club party in 1896. This will last far longer than any painting.

William Keith.

Photo courtesy National Park Service.
Photographer: Emily "Sissy" Hay

14

THE SIERRA CLUB IS BORN

The establishment of Yosemite Park delighted John Muir. The precious High Country would be saved. Yet Muir began to realize even more fully than before the tremendous forces against the park, against conservation, against wilderness. The battle had not been won, it had only been joined.

Often he felt very solitary in this fight. Yes, there were friends of his and friends of the wilderness. But there were not enough of them, and they skirmished alone and uncoordinated.

Meanwhile the exploitative spirit rolled on—the spirit that seemed to say: cut, burn, plow, graze, dam, mine, destroy! There's plenty more where that came from! The voices speaking for preservation, for husbanding resources that were rapidly diminshing, seemed weak, in spite of these fledgling and undefended national parks.

He came to feel that there must be an organization, there must be a concerted effort to maintain the gains that had been made.

At the same time an entirely different impulse led others in the same direction. A growing body of adventuresome hikers, many of them students or faculty members at the University of California and Stanford, wanted to explore the Sierra. Yet they had no maps. When they plunged into the mountains they could not learn from the experiences of those who had gone before. They could not tell which rivers to follow, which notches in the sky were truly passes, or what lay beyond the next ridge. They wanted more information.

One of these enthusiasts, Mr. Senger of San Francisco, conceived the idea of a mountaineering library with written accounts of the Sierra and maps of the region. It would be located in Yosemite Valley for the use of those who were heading into the back country.

Gradually, however, it became clear that the Bay Area would be a more central, accessible location for this material. Word began to go around that what was really needed was a mountaineering club—a Sierra club. Robert Underwood Johnson had been urging upon Muir the need for such an association to help in the preservation of California's natural wonders, especially Yosemite. A precedent existed in European alpine clubs, and in the Appalachian Club of the eastern United States.

This was far from being merely a student impulse. Some of the most prominent men (and a few women) of the Bay Area were beginning to think along these lines. They were not all acquainted, but they began to find each other.

William Keith's San Francisco studio became a focal point. Muir often made the journey from his ranch in Martinez to the studio to visit with his friend. Keith was a man of many talents, a most congenial person who drew people to him. When Muir arrived, Keith would see to it that others interested in nature, science, and the outdoors came to meet him. After talking at length, the friends would often drop down to a restaurant in the nearby California Market for lunch.

As this little nucleus of Keith, Muir, and Warren Olney drew about it an increasing number of like-minded citizens, they began to meet in Olney's law office at 101 Sansome Street. Among them were Professor Joseph Le Conte and others from the University of California, and David Starr Jordan, president of Stanford.

Muir was a pivotal member of these gatherings, and with his quiet but persuasive manner he sparked a growing enthusiasm for the enjoyment and defense of the mountains.

The incubation period shortly gave way to the birth of the new organization. On June 4, 1892, in Olney's office, the articles of incorporation of the club were drawn up and signed. John Muir was named president and Warren Olney first vice president, and a total of 182 charter members were soon enrolled.

The best-known section of the original articles of incorporation was Article III: "That the purposes for which this Corporation is formed are as follows, to-wit: To explore, enjoy and render accessible the mountain regions of the Pacific Coast; to publish authentic information concerning them; to enlist the support and co-operation of the people and government in preserving the forests and other natural features of the Sierra Nevada Mountains."

That night when he returned to his family in Martinez, John Muir was euphoric. Rarely had he seemed so ebullient, so overtly joyous. Now he had allies. He would no longer have to fight alone.

View across the meadows toward Cathedral Peak, from near Parsons Lodge and the Soda Springs.

15

EARLY CLIMBERS AND SURVEYORS

While cavalrymen were chasing sheepherders and making trails, the meadows also drew map-makers. In September 1878, the Wheeler Survey of the United States Army Engineers sent Lieutenant Macomb and topographer J. Calvert Spiller to Tuolumne Meadows. They climbed Dana, Conness, Cathedral Peak, and Mount Lyell. Heavy clouds about Lyell forced them to leave their work unfinished, so on the first of October, Macomb left Yosemite Valley, returned via Tuolumne Meadows to climb Mount Lyell a second time, and this time got the necessary surveying angles. The following day he hiked thirty-five miles back to the valley. Then, in spite of a heavy early snowstorm, Macomb and Spiller returned once again to climb Mount Hoffmann. The Wheeler Survey map of the Yosemite region was for years the standard, until superseded by that of François Matthes in the 1920s.

The next climbing season (1879) the United States Coast and Geodetic Survey sent a party under George Davidson to occupy 12,590-foot-high Mount Conness for measurements. In these rugged circumstances, and without benefit of today's nylon and down gear, they huddled on the summit and set to work. Each man served a stint of three days on top and then retreated to a recess below to recover. Often it snowed, and occasionally they were spooked off the peak by terrific thunderstorms. When, from distant Round Top to the east in Nevada, they finally received the signal to leave, they abandoned most of their equipment and plowed down to Mono Lake over snowdrifts ten feet deep.

Davidson and his men didn't return to Conness until 1887, and their longest stay was in 1890. As in 1869 (Muir's first Sierra summer), the latter was a stormy year. Almost every morning huge masses of cumulus clouds would begin to form, growing to tremendous heights before they enveloped the mountain tops and thunder deafened the beleaguered surveyors on their station in the sky. By evening the storms usually cleared, revealing blankets of fresh snow over everything. Later, under a star-studded sky, distant ranges shone in intricate detail.

Clarence King of the Whitney Survey became head of the United States Geological Survey in 1879, and appointed Israel C. Russell, Willard D. Johnson, and Grove Karl Gilbert to carry out an intensive study of the eastern slope between Mono Lake and Mounts Dana, Lyell, and Ritter. During the summers of 1882-83 they combed the area. Their findings appeared in Russell's impressive *Glaciers of North America*, published in 1897.

Perhaps the most daring act of the survey was Willard Johnson's descent into the bergschrund on Mount Lyell. Curious about how the ice and the rock wall joined, he had his companions lower him into the deep crevasse on a rope. A hundred and fifty feet down, he picked his way along the narrow corridor between glacier and mountain wall for about a hundred feet, crawling over masses of fallen rocks and chunks of ice as he clutched a sputtering candle under a continual rain from the melting ice walls.

There were also climbers in the meadows region in those years, though not necessarily the first. *The Climber's Guide to the High Sierra* speaks of "first ascents." But high on the peaks one can frequently pick up chips of worked obsidian which make it clear that Indians hunted far above timberline. We can assume that during ninety-six centuries, from time to time they ascended to the summits.

Then too, a widespread custom among many Indians in the Rockies and Great Plains, and perhaps at times among the Great Basin Paiute, was the spirit quest, a solitary journey into the wilderness or to a peak by a young man seeking a vision by which to live. He might build a commemorative cairn before returning to the human world below with his new knowledge and power. How many of the cairns we find today (often with a mountain register tucked among the rocks) had their origin in this way?

And yet, on many a mountain afternoon as we stand on a summit and feel we can touch the sky and reach out for a thousand miles, we

View across Garnet Lake. Mount Banner, right, is actually lower than Mount Ritter, left.

latterday questers also have our visions, and we too come down from the peaks stronger, wiser, and transfigured. Why else climb?

So for our region see Appendix 2 for a list of some of the first *recorded* climbs by a people who set great store by marks made in books.

With the exception of Muir, none of them left much description of their climbs. Helen Gompertz did. She had grown up in Berkeley as part of the group that included the Le Contes and the Keiths. Now an Oakland teacher, she was one of the six women charter members of the new Sierra Club.

In the summer of 1892 Helen and her friend, Isabel Miller, came to the meadows with G. M. Stratton, Joseph Le Conte, Jr. (called "Little Joe" for his scant five feet of height), and a burro named Jingle. Their objective: the summit of Mount Lyell.

When they reached the Soda Springs, John Lembert hailed them from the opposite bank of the Tuolumne River. He disappeared briefly to return with an ornery gray mule which he rode across the stream. Because of its vicious temper, Lembert warned them to mount it only on the right side.

Both women climbed on the undersized animal. "Now keep your feet up when you get to the middle of the stream," Lembert cautioned. While the men shouted, "Oh, for a kodak!" they made it across and pushed the dripping mule back into the water for a repeat performance with their companions.

"Arrived at the Spring," Helen wrote, "we prepared for a feast. So did the mosquitoes. Legions of them, bred in the wilderness and thirsting for human gore, feasted upon us so that we fled, completely routed, and rested not till we had put miles between us and our foes." It seems that over the years early summer conditions have not changed much in the meadows.

The next day they tramped up the Lyell Fork. Leaving Jingle staked out in a meadow, they pushed on to timberline, where they had a hard time collecting enough wood for a fire.

Five o'clock in the morning and bitter cold . . . They melted snow for coffee, and applied their kind of glacier cream: a thick layer of vaseline, smeared with soot from the base of the well-blackened coffee pot.

A three hour scramble up rocks and snow brought them to the moraine. In time they reached the glacier, where soon under intense Sierra sun they began to sink in at each step. They had to cut steps up the tongue of ice which in those days reached continuously from the glacier to the summit ridge. Finally "on the glorious summer day, July 9, 1892" they reached the top and its great view. Out came the coffee pot, a bag of pine chips for a fire, and lunch.

Eventually, an uproarious glissade all the way down to the rocks. Picking up their gear, they got back down to Jingle, "alive, but almost strangled in the coils of his long tether . . . we expressed our joy over his preservation by feeding him with old kid gloves and newspapers— dainty morsels, in his estimation."

Glorious summer days in and out of Tuolumne Meadows! Helen and Isabel were the first women on record to climb Lyell. Eleven years later, sprightly Helen and "Little Joe" were married.

Meanwhile, a new idea for enjoyment of the mountains was on its way. In 1884 a fourteen-year-old boy tending cattle near Fresno had gazed up at the gleaming serrated Sierra in the distance and envisioned a trail running along near the crest from end to end. His name was Theodore H. Solomons. "I could see myself in the immensity of that uplifted world," he wrote later, "an atom moving along just below the white, crawling from one end to the other of that horizon of high enchantment. It seemed a very heaven on earth for a wanderer."

The John Muir Trail had been conceived.

Four years later Solomons was in the high country on the first of many trips. In 1892 he and Joe Le Conte made a ten day journey to climb Mount Ritter. Between then and 1909 they had, with the help of others, charted most of the route of the present John Muir Trail along the backbone of the Sierra from Tuolumne Meadows to Mount Whitney.

Joseph LeConte, Jr. and Helen Gomperts.

Photo courtesy National Park Service

*Edward T. Parsons took this photo of an early Sierra Club
climbing party.*

16

COLBY AND PARSONS BLAZE A NEW KIND OF TRAIL: THE SIERRA CLUB OUTINGS

William Colby was nineteen in 1894 when he first came to Tuolumne Meadows. That summer he gulped it all down like strong drink: a quick dash up Mount Dana, a night shivering on top of Mount Conness, a descent down the Tuolumne Canyon. He came out of the mountains with a commitment that would last a long lifetime.

In the succeeding years Colby made endless hikes and climbs, and became a leader in the Sierra Club. He was elected secretary in 1901 and held that position for forty-six years, except between 1917 and 1919 when he was president. As a lawyer, he made a name in the field of mining law; he was also the first chairman of the California State Parks Commission.

It was way back in 1900 that Colby began to think of leading organized outings into the High Sierra. John Muir was enthusiastic for he believed that people should have the opportunity to go to the mountains and "get their good tidings." Colby was made chairman of the Outing Committee, and the first official Sierra Club Outing was scheduled for Tuolumne Meadows in the summer of 1901.

Just as plans were getting under way, a new member joined the club. Edward Parsons had risen from an impoverished childhood on a New York farm to become a successful businessman who traveled widely for his firm. In the course of his travels he fell in love with the mountains, joined the Mountaineers of Seattle, the Appalachian Mountain Club, and the Mazamas of Portland. With the Mazamas he helped to organize and lead large group climbs of the snow-capped northwest peaks. In Yosemite in 1900 he met John Muir, was deeply impressed, and joined the Sierra Club.

Edward Taylor Parsons on the trail.

As soon as Colby learned of Parsons's experience leading climbing groups he made him his right-hand man on the Outing Committee, a position he held for the next thirteen years. Together they led hundreds of people up mountains they would never otherwise have climbed.

Their routine was like a military operation whose rigid discipline would leave today's climbers gagging. After shoe inspection, as many as a hundred people would line up behind the leader at dawn. No one was to change places in line. At a slow, disciplined pace, the entire group would trudge up the approach slopes until they neared the summit. Then they would divide into smaller groups to help each other scramble to the top. Once off the summit, the line re-formed to return to camp. Colby and Parsons prided themselves on their safety record; due to their vigilance, climbs were seldom marred by mishaps.

Planning the first month-long outing for almost a hundred people, plus animals, packers, and cooks, was like planning an invasion. Campers brought cots and bedding (sleeping bags made by sewing quilts or blankets together, covered with denim). All wore hobnail boots, and the women sported short skirts (halfway between knee and ankle) with dark-colored bloomers beneath.

The leaders devised a special utensil patterned after the cup of the Appalachian Mountain Club: the Sierra Club Cup, which may be found by future archeologists in some mountain midden thousands of years after the club is long since forgotten.

That first summer the party of ninety-six assembled in Yosemite Valley. Joseph Le Conte, now full of years and honored by all, was present along with his family, rejoicing at the thought of returning once more to the meadows which had delighted him so long ago. But to the sadness of the entire group, he died quite suddenly of a heart attack before they left the valley. In spite of their sorrow the club members headed for Tuolumne Meadows. It took three days from the valley to get there. (Nowadays you can drive it in an easy hour and forty-five minutes.)

Once arrived in the meadows they established a base, Camp Muir, near the present-day bridge opposite Lembert Dome. From there, groups set out on demanding one-day expeditions to the surrounding mountains. Today Mount Dana is a six mile round trip from Tioga Pass, and a 3,000-foot climb. But to climb it they hiked twenty miles round trip and ascended 4,400 feet from Camp Muir.

As for Mount Lyell, twenty of the party left what is now called Lower Lyell Base Camp, climbed the mountain, and returned to Camp Muir in one long grueling day. Bloomers and riding breeches notwith-standing, they were durable. At the conclusion of the outing, the entire party hiked twenty-four miles over the Sunrise Trail to Yosemite Valley in one day.

From the beginning, the Sierra Club counted women among its members. In what was still the Victorian Age, Parsons wrote with solemn courtesy of these women, "Their vigor and endurance were a revelation to all of us." He soon married one of them, Marion Randall, a vivacious and gifted friend of John Muir's daughter, Wanda. She would go on many outings thereafter, and would be a director of the Sierra Club until 1938.

A hired crew did the packing, cooking, and cleanup under chief cook Charlie Tuck, a San Francisco Chinese who became a popular member of the outings. He came to love the club and the mountains. He once made a heroic all-night ride over Vogelsang Pass so that members of a side trip would not miss their breakfast. Another time, temporarily under the influence of the Demon Gin, he wandered about all night clad in a yellow slicker, and turned up sheepishly at camp in time for morning coffee. Charlie Tuck's camp stove turned out famously rib-sticking meals. Dinners were laid out in formal buffet, with eight women standing behind to serve in their best shirt-waists and long skirts, caps, aprons, and bandana kerchiefs.

The participants in the first outing were mostly professors, lawyers, college students, and businessmen on holiday: people who had the time, the money, and the inclination. They took nature seriously. Reading assignments were made before the start of the trip, and in camp there were natural history lectures by Muir and others around the evening fire. After it burned down, smaller parties drifted off to build dozens of tiny blazes for late night talk. The active social pro-gram included afternoon teas, singing, poetry readings, dancing the Virginia Reel, and skits.

These Sierra Club outings were to become a special kind of institu-tion in the Sierra. Many club members came back year after year, and life-long friendships developed among them. In time the High Trips (as they came to be called) camped throughout the range, crossed most of the high passes, and climbed most of the peaks. Yet, as Farquhar tells us, "Colby constantly reiterated that he and the other leaders could not afford to spend their time and energy merely giving people pleasant vacations; the important thing was to lead them to know and appreciate the beauty and inspiration of the mountains, and to educate them to become defenders of the wilderness. The results give ample testimony to the wisdom of this program."

Joseph Le Conte picnicking with his family shortly before his death.

Photo courtesy of National Park Service

William E. Colby, 1940.

Indeed, with changing times the results exceeded Colby's vision. The mountains did gain more and more defenders—eventually so many that impact became a problem. The club began to wonder about the injunction in their articles of incorporation, "to render accessible our mountain regions." By the 1940s the High Trips were using fewer mules and were avoiding the more fragile or heavily used areas. In the '60s the old time High Trips were discontinued altogether and replaced by High Light Trips limited to twenty-five members.

Meanwhile the by-laws have been changed, and the purpose of the club now reads, in part, "To explore, enjoy, and *preserve* our mountain regions." The club, however, has never ceased to honor William Colby for his early and sustained efforts to open up the mountains and bring appreciation of them to the many.

Club trips have now branched out into dozens of small excursions, not only in the Sierra but throughout the continent and the world. And it all began with that wonderful first Sierra Club Outing in Tuolumne Meadows in 1901.

17

THE SIERRA CLUB BUYS THE SODA SPRINGS, LOSES HETCH HETCHY, AND BUILDS PARSONS MEMORIAL LODGE

We now return to John Lembert lying murdered in his cabin in the Merced Canyon in the late 1890s. After he died his 160 acres at the Soda Springs passed to his brother, Jacob Lembert. He in turn sold it in 1898 to the McCauley brothers, one of whom, John, was proprietor of the hotel at Glacier Point. The brothers grazed cattle on the property and rented pasturage for the horses of passing visitors. They also built a cabin—the same rugged structure which is now a ranger residence.

When the McCauley heirs put the Soda Springs property on the market in 1912, William Colby took an option on the land. Even at this early date, he and other leaders of the club could sense the threat of development, and their purpose was to keep the meadows in its natural state. (As early as 1905, under pressure from mining interests and over club protest, the Ritter Range had been removed from the park, thus depriving it of much of its most spectacular scenery: Ritter, Banner, the Minarets, and also the beautiful Lakes Thousand Island, Garnet, and Ediza.)

Within a year the entire purchase price of the Lembert property had been raised by individual members' subscriptions. Now this already-historic site with its lovely meadow and commanding view of a turbulent sea of granite peaks belonged to the Sierra Club. However, from the very beginning, the club considered its ownership as a stewardship, not for its exclusive use, but for the enjoyment of all who should come that way.

The Soda Springs was safe, but another threat to their beloved wilderness loomed ahead. In 1907 the club outing included a visit to

Hetch Hetchy Valley. Considered by many a second Yosemite, this isolated region in the park had almost perpendicular walls, a floor grown to meadow and spreading oaks, and lovely waterfalls.

However, the city of San Francisco had recently suffered a drought which convinced many citizens that a new and more reliable water source must be found. They saw in Hetch Hetchy a great natural reservoir which only wanted damming. It was even suggested that Tuolumne Meadows itself could become a future reservoir, should Hetch Hetchy prove inadequate.

Most club members decried the idea. The winter after the outing, John Muir published in the Sierra Club Bulletin his famous article defending the threatened valley. The club directors and other conservationists joined him in proclaiming that it must be preserved.

Muir, Colby, and Parsons (along with many others) threw themselves into the fight to save Hetch Hetchy. Parsons published his photographs widely, and spent hours on the tedious and unglorious drudgery of letter writing, meetings, and committees. Muir contacted many people in high places who might help, and all three wrote repeatedly to President Roosevelt, to James Garfield, secretary of the interior, and to other mountaineering clubs, newspapers, and magazines.

The Sierra Club itself was almost torn apart by the struggle. Some of its most important members, including Warren Olney in whose office it had originally been organized, favored the dam. Charges and counter-charges were aired, as the internal struggle was blown up by the local press. After two years of controversy, in 1909 a mail ballot of all members revealed four to one in opposition to the dam.

In time Sierra Club members closed ranks on the Hetch Hetchy issue and worked actively as a group against the proposed dam. Colby in particular was indefatigable in writing, planning, meeting, and conferring. Over and over again they pointed out that the reservoir could just as well be placed lower down the Tuolumne Canyon outside the park, thus providing the needed water without ruining a scenic treasure. They must win! Hetch Hetchy was too valuable, too beautiful to lose. As Muir wrote, "Dam Hetch Hetchy! As well dam for water tanks the people's cathedrals and churches, for no holier temple has ever been consecrated by the art of man."

But the times were not on their side. The political forces at work were too strong for even the most devoted of conservationists. The more furiously they threw themselves against the gears of the machine, the more hopeless did it seem.

Hetch Hetchy Valley, pre-1913 (date unknown).

On December 17, 1913 the long fight was over. The Raker Act had passed through Congress and been signed into law by President Wilson. San Francisco was to have its water, and the magnificent Hetch Hetchy Valley was lost to future generations.

This was the Sierra Club's first great lost cause, and it exacted a heavy price. For within a few months Parsons suffered a heart attack, probably from disappointment and sheer exhaustion, and in May he died. John Muir wrote a glowing obituary for him. By the time it was published in the Sierra Club Bulletin of January, 1915, Muir himself was dead. Many said the Hetch Hetchy battle had killed him too.

The summer after these tragic deaths another Sierra Club Outing camped in the doomed Hetch Hetchy Valley. The club had been planning to build a lodge at the Soda Springs as a meeting place, reading room, and mountain headquarters. Drawings of the site plan and the building had already been made in 1913 in the office of Bernard Maybeck, a respected San Francisco architect, by his assistant, Mark White, a Sierra Club member. So at the meeting in Hetch Hetchy Valley it was proposed at the campfire one night that the lodge be dedicated to the memory of Edward Parsons.

The group also decided to ask the State of California to fund a memorial trail for John Muir, a trail to follow the Sierra crest from Yosemite Valley to Mount Whitney. In 1915 the state legislature voted $10,000 for the trail, and work was begun.

This would be a long effort. It was not until 1938 that the last section was completed—fifty-four years after Theodore Solomons first envisioned it from a cattle ranch down in the Central Valley.

As for Parsons Lodge, a substantial memorial fund was soon collected, including a fifty pound contribution by Edward Whymper, the famous British alpinist whose party first climbed the Swiss Matterhorn, and it was built in 1915. Engineer and climber Walter Huber planned the structural engineering, and Mark White worked with the park administration in supervising construction. It was decided to use native stone, making this the only building in the world of Johnson granite porphyry, an exceptionally fine-grained light rock. Hardware and cement were packed in on muleback as soon as the trails opened, and when the road was cleared, galvanized iron for the roof was brought by truck. The total cost was about three thousand dollars.

It's a gracefully proportioned building. While the style has been called "rustic," there are strong Mediterranean influences in the arched doorway, the stone-linteled windows, and the heavy walls which are

Parsons Lodge in 1931. It looks the same today.

three feet thick at ground level, tapering to two feet at the top. The sturdy door is bound with hand-wrought iron strap hinges and faced with galvanized iron. Window shutters are heavily studded with nails to make it bear-proof. At the rear is a massive stone fireplace, focus of animated conversation on numberless mountain summer evenings.

The lodge is now on the Register of National Historic Buildings. With the passing years the beauty of this simple building with its seemingly organic relationship to the surroundings has given visual pleasure to a multitude of visitors. It has served as a gathering place for generations of those who came like pilgrims to the mountains.

Photo courtesy of Bancroft Library, University of California at Berkeley.
Edward Taylor Parsons.

18

GRINNELL AND STORER: THE BIRDS AND THE BEASTS

It was a strange new salamander, and Tracy Storer and Joseph Grinnell were excited. They had found two of the tiny flat-headed creatures in a clump of heather below a snowbank on the slopes of Mount Lyell.

From a scientific viewpoint, "that was the greatest event of the entire survey," Storer wrote afterwards. It turned out to be even more unusual than they had first thought. The Mount Lyell salamander's only known relatives are in Sardinia, along the French and Italian rivieras, on the summit of Half Dome, and in the foothills of the Mother Lode.

At the time of this discovery Grinnell, the senior member of the party, was a well-known, somewhat formidable University of California zoologist, and Tracy Storer an earnest young graduate student at the same institution.

Grinnell had the idea of making a survey of all the vertebrates in a section across the Sierra Nevada, starting at an elevation of 250 feet at the base of the western foothills, moving up through the various life zones to 13,000 feet on Mount Lyell, then down to Mono Lake on the east side. He asked the Sierra Club for help. The members were enthusiastic and in the 1915 collecting season gave the survey the use of the club's pack train for hauling supplies.

Getting the pack animals to Tuolumne Meadows was a rugged job, for as usual the "road" was only a poorly marked route. When the survey party made it, they set up a base camp at the Soda Springs. By mid-June a collecting station had been established at the head of Lyell Canyon. On June 18 the group started out to climb the mountain and found their precious salamander.

The University of California Survey was fairly elaborate with no fewer than forty collecting stations all together, mostly managed by students. The field work started in November, 1914, and continued off and on through 1920. The result was the publication of *Animal Life in the Yosemite*. All present-day animal research in Yosemite starts with this book.

Grinnell and Storer and their colleague, Joseph Dixon, found most of the same animals and birds in the meadows area that we see today— with some interesting exceptions. For example, the cowbird, quite common now, is not native but came in with the construction of the stables. Steller's jays, the most audacious camp robbers, have come up from lower elevations since the days of the survey, more or less re-placing in that role the Clark's nutcrackers, who used to follow the sheep and have now moved back to near-timberline. And at Mono Pass today you may find the white-tailed ptarmigan introduced as a game bird on the east slope, but now coming over the crest.

Along the river and at the Soda Springs were spotted sandpipers bobbing up and down, nervous killdeer, pine siskins, and California gulls. The gulls nest at Mono Lake, but the lake is too salty to drink. So they zoom up for sips of mountain water and perhaps some fishing. Occasionally the survey would hear a rattling kingfisher, or by rapids and falls meet the water ouzel who inspired one of Muir's finest essays.

In ponds and marshes were redwinged blackbirds and mallards. Out in the meadows the survey found mountain bluebirds of unearthly hue, robins, Brewer's blackbirds, the sweet-voiced Cassin's finch, acro-batic violet-green and tree swallows, chipping and white-crowned sparrows. (Occidental College, in the footprints of Grinnell and Storer, has been studying the white crowns of the Tioga Pass region every summer since 1968.)

Colorful western tanagers, evening and pine grosbeaks, yellow-rumped warblers, and red crossbills flashed through the woods. Jun-cos and chickadees were everywhere, with white-breasted nuthatches coming down tree trunks while brown creepers went up. Pine trees often reverberated with the hammering of hairy woodpeckers, flickers, Williamson's sapsuckers, and even sometimes the rather rare black-backed three-toed woodpecker. From deeper in the forest as twilight fell they would hear the enchanting flute-like voice of the hermit thrush.

A climb up Dana carried them through zones of rufous humming-birds zinging around blue larkspur and red paintbrush, kestrels hawking after fat grasshoppers, and on the alpine fell fields, horned larks and the musical rock wren. Gray crowned rosy finches would guide them to the very summit. This most charming Sierra bird thinks it's all roses on mountain tops and eats insects off snow fields. He accepts mountain climbers as his equals, often sitting down to lunch with them before zooming over the cliff edge to his nest in some inaccessible cranny.

Over those vast mountain spaces they probably spotted a pair of soaring red-tailed hawks or grander yet, golden eagles.

These are but a sample of the bird life which Grinnell and Storer found enlivening the high country.* Now, as then, a worthwhile day trip out of the meadows is down to Mono Lake. There one can easily add several dozen more species to his high country list: phalaropes, grebes, avocets, coots, to name a few.

The mountain summer is short, only a matter of weeks. In that time the birds and most animals mate, nest, and raise their young with incredible speed. Golden mantled ground squirrels, chipmunks, and Belding's ground squirrels seldom stop their furious round. Voles and mice are more elusive. A flash along the ground and they're gone. No wonder, for we also have weasels, wonderfully efficient hunters. There are badgers, too, seldom seen though they have pocked the meadows with their wide-mouthed burrows.

Pikas, small round-faced rodents with high whistly voices, feel at home among the talus on mountainsides along with the golden marmot, usually basking on a rock in the sun in preparation for his long winter hibernation. The porcupine, by contrast, hangs out in the woods and leaves his tooth-marks on many a lodgepole pine. The pointy-eared chickaree has a big voice for a little squirrel, and complains loudly at your invasion of his territory.

The Yosemite toad lives only along the spine of the Sierra. It hibernates from September until early summer. The year-round climate of Tuolumne Meadows suits it just fine. Thumb-sized hyla frogs are favorites with children.

---

*For years the Sierra Club kept a list in Parsons Lodge of the species of birds sighted at the Soda Springs. In recent years Michael Ross, naturalist, has totaled up sixty-nine bird species seen in the meadows. For the wider Tuolumne area, ornithologist David Gaines's indispensable book, *Birds of Yosemite*, shows many more.

Aquatic garter snakes are the most frequent reptiles. Rattlesnakes have been found in the meadows, but very rarely.

Grazing deer and foraging coyotes are familiar sights. Along the trails, if you are very quiet and very lucky, you may see a martin. And last but not least, there's the famous (or infamous) black bear.

Grinnell, Storer, and Dixon remained active in the investigation of Sierra Nevada animal life. In 1963 Storer wrote *Sierra Nevada Natural History*. He lived into his eighties, respected and revered as one of the great students of nature in the Sierra. But perhaps his most public act was to design the grizzly bear emblem for the California state flag. The California grizzly is long extinct, but the flag waves on.

Photo courtesy of National Park Service

Mount Lyell salamander.

19

STEVE MATHER BUYS THE TIOGA ROAD
AND THROWS A PARTY

Yosemite Park existed. The law said it did. The army had defended it, the sheepmen had painfully learned to avoid it, and civilian rangers were trying to patrol it. Congress had even allotted it a pittance.

By 1914 in addition to Yosemite and Yellowstone there were eleven other national parks and eighteen national monuments. They were variously managed and mismanaged, as they had never been unified under a single administration. Pressure had grown to create a Bureau of National Parks. Finally in 1913 Interior Secretary Franklin K. Lane had set up an office of the parks within his department.

Nevertheless, with the disheartening loss of Hetch Hetchy conservationists had come to realize that the fight to protect these national treasures would never be permanently won. Just as the onslaughts against them would be unremitting, there must be eternal vigilance to preserve them. John Muir, the lone evangelist coming down from the mountains to preach a new religion (wilderness), was dead. Now the religion had been institutionalized into a system of national parks. Where was the leader who would combine Muir's evangelical fervor with executive ability?

In the summer of 1914 Stephen Tyng Mather visited a number of the new national parks and was distressed at the shoddy administration he observed. Being a man of action, he sat down and wrote to his old college friend, Secretary Lane. Lane wrote back that if he didn't like how the parks were run, he should come to Washington and run them himself.

Lane knew his man. Mather accepted. At forty-seven, this descendant of Increase and Cotton Mather, graduate of the University of California at Berkeley, was a wealthy borax tycoon in Chicago, and a distinguished philanthropist. He loved the Sierra and had joined the Sierra Club in 1904, going on many of their outings. Now he had an itch to serve the cause of conservation in a bigger way. He had boundless energy, loved people, and could have sold an ice box to an Eskimo. Above all, he could afford to take a job at stenographer's pay and yet travel and entertain like a prince.

He signed on for one year, and stayed fourteen, until shortly before his death in 1930. During those vital fourteen years Mather gave shape and consistency to the administration of the parks. He laid down most of the policies and precedents that govern them today. Supersalesman that he was, he sold the parks to the Congress and to the American people. While battling the forces that would destroy or exploit them, he spent lavishly of his own money for their improvement. He gave rangers and administrators a sense of common purpose and esprit de corps. And he left a heritage that millions of Americans benefit from today.

Mather had a great impact on his favorite park, Yosemite, and on its Tuolumne Meadows region. Back in 1914 getting to the high country was not easy. The only "thoroughfare" was the Tioga Road, fifty-six miles of boulders, fallen logs, and erosion gullies, still in private hands, and a toll road at that.

Mather determined to repair it, but could do nothing unless the government owned it. All right, he would buy it himself and donate it to the people.

It was gently pointed out to him that by law Congress must scrutinize every gift. Presents to the government cannot be accepted lightly. Fitzgerald, chairman of the Appropriations Committee, was sure only skulduggery would prompt such an offer. Only by conniving with some like-minded senators could Mather finally prevail on the committee to give him the go-ahead.

The purchase price was $15,500.00. Mather raised about half of this by subscriptions of wealthy patrons, and contributed the balance himself. By a single act of personal generosity he was to make Tuolumne Meadows accessible to a much larger public. The automobile clubs, who had long been advocating a route over the Yosemite Sierra, now repaired it in short order.

To the experienced mountain driver with ice water in his veins, the approach to the Tioga Road up the eastern escarpment from Lee

Tioga Road descending Lee Vining Canyon, 1920s.

Vining was simply a thrilling experience. But to the uninitiated from the flatlands it was scary as hell! Barely one car wide, it snaked without guardrails along a mountain wall that dropped dizzily a couple of thousand feet into space. Yet the year of its completion (1916) was also the year of two international expositions in California, and tourists streamed over it. Many found their drive through the High Sierra the most hair-raising part of their entire trip.

It was also in 1916 that Mather made his first official mountain visit as director of the national parks, and he came to Tuolumne Meadows. This was not just a tour of inspection and not just a lark, though it was something of both. It was a proselytizing tour de force. Those who were lucky enough to come along were carefully selected: editors, writers, heads of important committees, president of the National Geographic Society, and other "movers and shakers." These were the people who could do the most to promote our national parks, and he wanted them to become intimately acquainted with some of them. They did.

But not by dint of austerity. That, Mather reasoned, could be counter-productive. He spent some four thousand dollars of his own money for the two week trip for the four hosts (Mather, Daniels, and Albright of the park service, and Marshall of the geological survey) and their fifteen captive luminaries, as well as packers and Ty Sing, a celebrated trail cook. They had all the back country luxuries: horses, air mattresses, and generous supplies of fresh fruits and vegetables.

Ty turned out endless epicurean repasts with steak and trout, venison and chicken, pies and cakes, plum puddings and fresh rolls, all served on clean linen. He used to start the bread dough in the morning and pack it in a mule kayak to rise as it rode against the mule's warm body through the day. Disaster struck one day when the mule rolled over and spread yeasty paste across an alpine meadow—a mess, it was reported, that would have sickened a seagull. (Later the geological survey named a mountain for this cook: Mount Sing in the southeast part of Yosemite National Park.)

Mather's route went through Sequoia Park to Mount Whitney, which most of the party climbed. Then they drove north to Mono Lake, up the Lee Vining Creek Road to the eastern boundary of Yosemite National Park, down the newly repaired Tioga Road through Tuolumne Meadows, and back to Yosemite Valley.

His guests were eminent, but not all were outdoorsmen. Two of the party chickened out before they started, scared off by teasing tales of human bones bleaching along the trails. Two others wore heavy black

Stephen T. Mather, founder of the National Park Service.

veils over their hats, claiming they were sensitive to black flies, "of which we saw none."

Mather, the eternal fraternity boy, loved skinny-dipping under waterfalls, and never passed one up without shouting, "Here we get a free shower!" He would leap off his horse along with a few other masochists, strip down, and plunge into the icy water, whooping and hollering with delight.

He could not stand inaction and, unlike many mountain-lovers, disliked solitude. When in camp he was always the first one up, and could not rest until everyone else was, too—even if it meant letting the air out of their mattresses, beating on pans, and shrieking like an Indian raiding party. He was indefatigable on the trail. After a hard day's climb, with everyone else slumped by the fire in stuporous weariness, Mather was ready to sit up half the night talking about the parks, or planning future expeditions.

On that trip the most prideful achievement may have been climbing Mount Whitney, but the most blood-curdling trial was the ascent of the Lee Vining Road to the park entrance at 10,000 feet. They had hired some natives to drive, one of whom, after a brief glance ahead, would rise up and turn around, waving one hand and declaiming on the view. His passengers were speechless with terror. One later wrote, "Albright was trying to keep one hand on the open door and one foot on the running board and at the same time to hold off Hough, who was clawing at him and hoarsely whispering over and over, 'Goddam that scenery-loving cuss, god*dam* that scenery-loving cuss!'"

They spent their last high night camping with the Sierra Club at the Soda Springs. Over a campfire they were able to review the fabulous trip, which had been an eye-opener to all of them.

Here at the same Soda Springs where so many years before Muir and Johnson had dedicated themselves to creating Yosemite National Park, there was an implicit rededication to all the parks. Mather's effort and expense had not been in vain. Each one of his guests went on to write about, defend, subsidize, and extoll these national treasures.

But then, that was Mather's way: to serve mightily himself, and to galvanize others into doing so. The bronze plaques memorializing Mather which can be found in many national parks and monuments say it well:

"There will never come an end to the good that he has done."

20

FRANÇOIS MATTHES READS THE ROCKS AND THE NATURE GUIDES TELL THE STORY

Nowadays on Tuolumne rambles when a ranger says, "The Lyell Glacier flowed here," or, "Cathedral Peak was never covered by ice," few of us realize the study that went into deciphering the landscape's coded messages so that the story could be told. In our mountains the chief decoder was a Dutch-American, François Emile Matthes.

François and his twin brother, Gerard, were born in Amsterdam in 1874 into a wealthy and distinguished Dutch family. They spent much of their boyhood in the Swiss Alps, attended a German technical high school, were tutored in art (at which François showed great talent), and traveled widely in Europe. They had planned to go on to a German university, but a chance meeting with an American professor caused them to decide on Massachusetts Institute of Technology. There they took the geodetic course and both graduated with honors. The next year they became American citizens.

Gerard went on to become a well-known hydrographic engineer. François joined the United States Geological Survey and in 1898 was sent out to survey in Indian Territory, now Oklahoma. Later he was to work in the Bighorns in Wyoming and the Montana Rockies. His photographs and publications about the latter were influential in the establishment of Glacier National Park.

The cultured European had become a seasoned wilderness traveler, as adept at wrangling pack stock as at operating an alidade and plane table. He spent two years under incredibly difficult conditions surveying part of the Grand Canyon. On this and other assignments he combined the skills of a meticulous scientist with those of a creative artist to produce topographic maps of surpassing accuracy and elegance.

In 1903 he visited Yosemite Valley and fell in love with it. When in 1905 he was asked by the geological survey to make a large-scale map of Yosemite Valley, he jumped at the chance.

In 1911 he married an American, Edith Coyle. From the beginning Edith followed him around the west. She rode and climbed with him, and served as chauffeur, secretary, and chief of commissary on pack trips. When he was working along the east front of the Sierra she spent many an evening at lonely roadheads waiting for his return, with the car doors locked and a geologist's pick beside her as a weapon.

As he created his maps Matthes had become ever more fascinated by the landforms he was delineating, and had turned to the study of geology for better understanding. His last big topographic job was Mount Rainier. Then in 1913 he transferred from the topographic to the geologic branch of the geological survey.

The Sierra Club had been urging the survey to make a systematic study of the geologic history of the Yosemite region, and Matthes's first geologic assignment was to study the origins of Yosemite Valley and to report his findings "in language understandable . . . to any intelligent and interested readers." Frank C. Calkins was to work with him, studying the rocks. Their work continued for sixteen long years as they poked about valleys, measured glaciers, and mapped ancient streambeds, extending their investigations up the Merced and Tuolumne basins and along the crest of the range.

In time Matthes produced the Yosemite Valley Sheet, a masterpiece of accuracy, almost a relief map. Even the overhangs on cliffs were shown. He then went on to work out the history of the entire region.

Often during these years Matthes was in and out of Tuolumne Meadows. No one before or since has scrutinized so minutely the manuscript of its rocks and streams, its domes and peaks and faces. He came to understand as no one before him the processes which made the mountains as we see them today.

In the meadows region he made a first ascent of Vogelsang Peak some time before 1923, and he gave the Cockscomb its name. (A nearby spectacular granite spine was named Matthes Crest to memorialize him after his death.) As he pursued his work he contributed essays to the Sierra Club Bulletin describing his findings. One of the most charming of these is "The Little Lost Valley of Shepherd's Crest," describing in his magically simple prose the lowland valley that, as the

Geologist François Matthes.

Sierra rose into the sky, was carried upward above the line of glaciation and survives to this day as a high alpine relic of an earlier age, just north of Mount Conness.

Finally in 1930 Matthes published his *Geologic History of Yosemite* (Professional Paper No. 160), a book so fine that it immediately became a classic of scientific writing. Many a well-known climber has carried it along in his pack, and today it is a collector's item.

In Yosemite, his talks on the history of the region were spellbinders, for not only was he an accomplished writer, but a skilled teacher and speaker as well.

Matthes's interests had taken him from map-making to landforms, and then to glaciation, and he made outstanding contributions in each field. He supervised a plan for studies and measurements of glaciers in the United States and elsewhere, through which more became known about prehistoric climates.

After some years away from the Sierra he returned in 1935 to Sequoia National Park, and to Yosemite during the spring, summer, and fall from 1936 to 1939, studying the east slope of the range. He suspected that it was of much more recent origin than had been previously thought, and produced convincing evidence to support this view. These were his last visits to Tuolumne Meadows.

In 1948 the Department of the Interior awarded him its gold medal for fifty-one years of distinguished service.

It was his dream to devote his retirement years to a more comprehensive and definitive book about the Yosemite region, but that was not to be. He died shortly after retirement, at age seventy-four, just as he was getting down to work on his long-planned volume. Afterwards his wife and his friend Fritiof Fryxell collected Matthes's extant Yosemite writings into *The Incomparable Valley*, illustrated by Ansel Adams. A beautiful and lucid work, it must console us for the monumental volume which Matthes did not live to write.

Although Matthes's writing has thus reached a wide public, too often the findings of other scholars are buried in university libraries remote from most people. Now for Yosemite something occurred which was to change that.

About the time Matthes and Calkins were beginning their study, a Mr. and Mrs. C. M. Goethe of Sacramento were traveling around the world, noting with fascination how various European nations included nature study in their educational systems.

Back in California, the Goethes financed an enormously successful nature guide program at Lake Tahoe for the University of California. This soon caught the eye of Stephen Mather. At the time he was engaged in controversy with certain amusement companies who wanted to make Yosemite into a huge and profitable Coney Island complete with hot dog stands and jangling ferris wheels. Mather felt that a nature guide program would be the best answer to this kind of nonsense, and he persuaded Dr. Harold C. Bryant and Dr. Loye Miller to move the Tahoe program for the following summer to Yosemite Valley. There was no money, so with the help of the Fish and Game Commission, Mather and Goethe again dug deep and paid the bill.

The response was tremendous. In 1925, Dr. Bryant expanded it into the Yosemite Field School for the park service; it met each summer in Yosemite Valley. Dr. Bryant was a dedicated nature crusader who wanted everyone to experience the mountains to the fullest, and the final week of each session was spent in Tuolumne Meadows and its back country.

The field school thrived for many years, finally closing in 1954. During its life it prepared many of the outstanding ranger naturalists of Yosemite and other national parks. They have become a loved and respected part of American life, interpreting for thousands what Matthes and his fellow scientists, often working almost alone, had discovered.

21

THE TWENTIES IN THE MEADOWS

In the mountains the Roaring Twenties passed serenely. The only flaming youth Tuolumne Meadows knew were campers singed by their campfires. The only roaring, the river loud with snowmelt. Now and then one heard the gentle tapping of François Matthes's geologist's hammer.

Numbers of automobile tourists came to camp in Tuolumne Meadows, and others packed into the back country. Each season there were Sierra Club High Trips, often starting and ending in the meadows. And the High Sierra Camps came into being.

Back in 1916 concessioner D. J. Desmond had built Tuolumne Meadows Lodge and Tenaya and Merced Lake camps. Somewhat pretentiously called "mountain chalets," each camp had one canvas-roofed stone building for dining room and kitchen, and canvas tents for guests who paid three dollars a day for lodging, breakfast, and dinner.

The camps were closed by Desmond's bankruptcy in 1918, but in 1924 they were reopened, and the Yosemite National Park Company (shortly to become Yosemite Park and Curry Company) built Glen Aulin and Vogelsang camps. The May Lake Camp was opened in 1938 to replace the old Tenaya Lake Camp, which was closed that year. Finally in 1961 the Sunrise High Sierra Camp, entirely financed by Mary Curry Tressider, completed the string. Ranger naturalists often lead parties along this delightful high country loop. It has been immensely popular over the years—a way for non-backpackers to have a back country experience.

Tioga Pass Road Opening, June 3, 1928. Mount Dana in background.

In the twenties the deer population presented a new threat: they were infected with hoof and mouth disease. This was partly a response to overpopulation, for predators which had helped to keep their numbers in balance had themselves been relentlessly hunted and reduced. The disease spread rapidly among the crowded and starving animals, and soon threatened cattle on lands adjacent to the park.

Pressure was put upon Stephen Mather to order the destruction of the diseased deer. He was horrified. He loved all animals and even frowned on the shooting of predators, which was commonly accepted in his time. However, he finally consented, and in 1924 the great kill proceeded. Twenty thousand deer were ultimately destroyed, and the disease was eradicated. The remaining healthy deer have, since then, been so successful that their increase is of continuing concern to park specialists in wildlife management.

During the First World War there had been agitation to let sheep back into the park, on the grounds of patriotic necessity, to produce wool and meat for the army. President Wilson even grazed sheep on the White House lawn as a demonstration. Mather (and, in his temporary absence, Albright) was hard put to counter the pressure, for wool growers did not easily resist the financial enticement of practically free pasture. Finally Interior Secretary Lane ordered Albright to wire the park permission to let in 50,000 sheep. "But don't let the Sierra Club find out," he added. While Albright stalled, the club did find out, drew itself up into battle array, and alerted sympathetic congressmen. Lane withdrew the order, and Tuolumne Meadows was saved once again.

Now in the '20s the sheepherders were back on their side of the boundary, and there was no longer a state of hostility. In his memoirs, ex-ranger Bingaman tells of a Basque who regularly invited him over the line for coffee and sheepherder bread, a redolent sourdough, while they smiled at each other past their language barrier, and shared a silent smoke.

Sometimes there were problems with people. Even this peaceful mountain landscape saw an occasional Bad Guy. One August afternoon in 1921, a masked bandit held up the manager of the Tenaya Lake High Sierra Camp at gunpoint, took $350, and made a getaway. Rangers and the trail crew foreman searched all night and all the next day with no luck.

Some years later the bandit was picked up on another count in Oregon and confessed the job at Tenaya Lake. He told how he had worked his way down the trail to the valley, hiding in the brush as his searchers went by, and had slept the night among the pioneers in the Yosemite cemetery.

So much for the Lawless West in the Yosemite High Sierra.

It was during the '20s too that the meadows saw the grand finale of one of the Sierra's great solo adventures. On Christmas Day of 1928 Orland Bartholomew, former stream gauger for California Edison Company, left Big Creek, California and headed up Cottonwood Canyon on skis. On April Fool's Day, 1929, he skied down from Donohue Pass, along the Lyell Canyon, through the meadows, and back to civilization in Yosemite Valley. Alone, he had made the first winter ascent of Whitney. Swinging with fair weather and foul, crossing thirteen precipitous snowbound passes, and threatened by thundering avalanches, he had traversed more than the entire length of the John Muir Trail, spent forty-two nights above 10,000 feet in temperatures which dropped as low as fourteen degrees below zero, covered more than three hundred miles, mostly on skis, and climbed and descended more than 70,000 vertical feet. No one since has matched his lonely, grueling exploit.

During these years a young pianist and photographer was hiking and photographing along the back country trails of Yosemite and points south, sometimes with violinist Cedric Wright, or with Little Joe Le Conte and his family, or sometimes alone with a mule and a camera. His name: Ansel Adams. His whole life would be a celebration of the beauty of the natural world, and his photographs would in time prove to be one of the most eloquent voices for its preservation.

It has always been a struggle to preserve beauty from the insatiable maw of utility. Today we read with horror that in 1921 a vigorous effort was made to push through a road from Happy Isles in Yosemite Valley, up the Merced Canyon past Vernal and Nevada falls, over Forsyth Pass, and down to Tenaya Lake. Praise be, Congress did not see fit to fund it.

What then passed as "progress" would have been one of those irreversible acts like the building of O'Shaughnessy Dam in the Hetch Hetchy, or the destruction of Glen Canyon. Once done, that shining trail up Little Yosemite, which lifts the hiker's spirits in a way no road can do, would have been lost as wilderness.

Pack train crossing Tuolumne Meadows, September 1923.

22

CARL SHARSMITH, THE MEADOWS' FIRST RANGER NATURALIST

During the depression things were tough down at sea level. But if you could manage some cheap gas to get to the mountains you could live on a shoestring. In the campground there were no time limits and no fees. And in the meadows you would find a guide to make your high country experience unforgettable: Carl Sharsmith.

Some time before the First World War, Carl came with his parents from Switzerland to the United States, and eventually to southern California. "Since school was nothing but fighting," he says, "I quit in the seventh grade and went to work." In the ensuing years he worked sometimes as a miner and sometimes as a logger. He learned great respect for the loggers, many of them real woodsmen who passed on to him their rich lore of the ways of the woods. By 1920, when he was seventeen, he had started climbing. That year he climbed the north side of Mount Shasta, alone.

Now he wanted more—he wanted to complete his education. So at twenty-one he entered the ninth grade at Le Conte Junior High School in Los Angeles.

Although he felt socially isolated among the younger students, a wonderful thing happened in his life. He had read Muir's essay, "The Bee-Pastures." One weekend he set out for the foothills to find them, and along the way he encountered a boys' organization called the Trail-finders. He joined the group and in time became one of their leaders. From then on, while he continued through high school and into college, each summer he was out leading the boys on Sierra pack trips.

He had the idea of starting in the south and working north, crossing the range by every route from east to west and west to east. By the summer of 1930 he had almost completed this objective.

That year he heard about the Yosemite Field School and applied. Although he was twenty-seven years old, he had not yet finished college, and the directors may have looked askance at his odd educational history. Still, his grades were excellent and his recommendations glowing. They put him down as an alternate. As it turned out, someone else dropped out and he was accepted.

It was obvious from the beginning that he had a deep love of the mountains, an extraordinary depth of outdoor experience, and a way with people. Halfway through the session he was asked to join the park service for the following summer as a ranger naturalist. Fifty years later Carl can say, "I was very pleased." In 1931 he was stationed in Tuolumne Meadows, the first of its ranger naturalists, and for some time the only one.

The meadows had received their most passionate advocate, their most steadfast friend, since John Muir.

It was hard work, but this slight, cheerful young Swiss-American shouldered it all with a will. There were flower walks and mountain climbs, fire-fighting and campground patrol. After a long full day he would hold a campfire at which he would tell animal stories and Indian stories, even do Indian dances. Afterwards he might get out his accordion and lead off with a few songs.

"I've a picture of me in front of my tent," he muses, and pulls on his pipe. "Oh, I looked cocky, with knickers and knee socks, and my hat at just the right jaunty angle. And there was a little tree knee-high beside me. Do you know, that tree's grown up and shades the whole tent now!"

At that time the campground was gloriously informal, more an idea than a thing. Carl would ride his horse up and down the river in the morning, seeing who was camped where, and not averse to accepting a fresh camp biscuit with blackberry jam and a steaming cup of coffee. He was welcome at all hearths, for even his admonitions were gentle: "Be sure to put your fire out when you leave. Be careful not to walk on the flowers."

Carl opened other people's eyes to the world around them—and constantly opened his own eyes to see, to experience the mountains in all of their moods, to contemplate all of their faces. It all pulsated with beauty and mystery that he longed to penetrate more deeply.

His first love had been geology, but he found himself drawn ever

Carl Sharsmith leading a group on Mount Conness in 1932.

more irresistibly toward botany. "It's not one or the other," he says, "they all go together." He was fascinated by the relationships between plants and animals and soils, and especially by plants wordlessly making the world green and the air pure. As he studied the grasses he made himself into a range ecologist, and as he studied the flowers he became a taxonomist. His doctoral dissertation at the University of California at Berkeley was, quite naturally, about the alpine flora of the Sierra.

He had a rich double life. In the winters he taught, first at Washington State, then the University of Minnesota, and finally for the longest period at San Jose State University in California. In the summers, as a ranger naturalist, he taught in a different way, as hikers toiled after him, breathless with the altitude and the effort to catch each soft-spoken word.

This was the life that Carl wanted to live, rooted in the meadows like the young pine tree that has grown older with him. "No preacher preaching hell fire and damnation was ever more fiery or more sincere than I was," he reminisces. "I wanted everyone to experience the mountains in every way. I wanted to mountainize the whole world!"

In those days as in our own, part of a ranger's job was mountain rescue. Some of these efforts ended tragically, for the mountains are often unforgiving when humans make mistakes. Some were exasperating, such as when, after beating the bushes for days for a missing fisherman, they heard he had gone on to Lake Tahoe. And there were those wonderful times when a lost child was restored unhurt to its parents, or a husband to his wife.

One of the noteworthy mountain rescues of the '30s—and it did end happily—was when Carl Sharsmith himself fell off the top of Mount Maclure and had to be rescued.

In 1935 he had led a Yosemite Field School group up Mount Lyell and then, with a few others, had gone on to climb nearby Mount Maclure.* The rest started back down Lyell toward camp. On Maclure it was a beautiful day, and perhaps Carl may have been a little over-confident. Somehow he moved too close to a rotten edge. Suddenly the rock gave way and he was thrown backwards and began to somersault

---

*In the first edition of this book I assumed this peak was named for Lieutenant N. F. McClure and spelled it accordingly. Mr. N. King Huber, Park Geologist, has kindly informed me that the peak was named Mount Maclure by J. D. Whitney by 1868 in honor of "a pioneer in American geology."

over and over down a chute before his horrified companions. Bounding after him, they found him semi-conscious, caught in a hollow with his feet dangling over a 1,500-foot cliff, and bleeding from an ugly gash on the head. Someone found some black button thread to sew up the head wound, while word was sent ahead for help. The only possible way to get him back to camp was to carry him in a hastily improvised rope sling back to the summit of Maclure, then down to the Lyell Glacier and across it.

In his state of shock he was chilled to the bone. It had grown dark by the time they carried him across the deeply pitted glacier on a stretcher made of two crooked sticks and a blanket, and each time one of the bearers slipped and went down, Carl was slammed against the frozen snow.

He noticed they were going wrong. "Farther to the left, farther to the left, there's a gap in the moraine where you can get through," he protested. But they ignored him, thinking he was out of his head.

Word of the accident was quickly relayed to the camp below. Some members of the group prepared food and carried it up to feed the party. Others hauled up wood and lit fires at intervals on the glacier to make a path of light. One headed for the meadows to telephone for an ambulance to be sent from Yosemite Valley. Around midnight the rescue group reached Upper Lyell Base Camp, and early the next morning they commenced carrying him down the trail. On the floor of the canyon they were met by a Civilian Conservation Corps crew who brought him in to the waiting ambulance.

After two months in the hospital, Carl emerged feeling that he had truly been granted a second life. The next season, and for many years thereafter, he was climbing Lyell and Maclure, without even a scar to show for his ordeal. We will meet him again, for his history and that of the meadows have flowed together, two streams that mingled. No one in the past has ever spent as many years there; probably no one will again.

Photo courtesy of National Park Service
Carl Sharsmith

23

MORE TALES OF THE THIRTIES

These were the days when the visitor's first challenge was to get to the meadows. The Tioga Road, still more an obstacle than a thoroughfare, was all dirt until 1937. In the fall of that year the stretch from Cathedral Creek to Tioga Pass was paved, as was the section from Crane Flat to the White Wolf turnoff in 1939.

Between these two, the Twenty-one Mile Stretch of Blessed Memory remained essentially unchanged for nearly a quarter of a century. Narrow, winding, mean and ornery to drive, it snaked around every tree bole and granite boulder and up and down every rise and drop, and truly constituted a baffle between the high country and civilization.

The Civilian Conservation Corps came in 1933. They built the Visitors' Center at the campground entrance—built it of granite and logs with a steep shake roof and a big fireplace. For almost fifty years it would welcome pilgrims, looking exactly the way a visitors' center should look. It was finally closed in 1980 and the center moved west a couple of miles to the larger old CCC mess hall.

The National Park Service and the CCC built the new campground which officially opened in 1936, with impresssive stone restrooms and about three hundred sites—a gigantic complex for those days, yet hidden in the woods in such a way that it has never lessened the visual beauty of the meadows. Now one more era had passed, for no longer could people camp up and down the meadows and along the river at will. Many old-timers mourned abandoning sites they had used for twenty or thirty years, and had thought of as their own.

Meanwhile life in the Sierra Club campground at the Soda Springs went on. In the mid-'30s one of the memorable custodians was a gre-

Road work on Tioga Road near Tuolumne Ranger Station, June 1931.

garious bachelor named Albert Dühme, a great camp cook who grew stout on his own creations. He put on potlucks, campfire programs, and flower walks, and occasionally threw a steak dinner for the rangers. His most notable contribution was the Bruin Baffle, a sturdy building with a galvanized iron door, where members could stow their grub safe from marauding bears.

The Sierra Club outings were now a venerable tradition. Large parties, often with stock and packers, frequently used the Soda Springs campground as their starting or finishing point. Since Muir's day few had explored the Grand Canyon of the Tuolumne. Many years of high water prevented passage through. But in 1931 the water was low, and an outing made a grand loop down the Tuolumne Canyon, north to the Matterhorn country, and back to Soda Springs; then another loop south to the Minarets and back again. Parsons Lodge echoed to many a tale of mountain wanderings.

Sometimes the stories were of botanical finds. In 1933, Dr. Carlton Ball of the University of California Herbarium set out to track down a tiny alpine willow, *Salix nivalis*. It had never been seen in California, but he had a hunch it was lurking somewhere above 10,000 feet around Mount Dana. The search was arduous, but finally one night in Parsons Lodge Dr. Ball triumphantly waved aloft a precious thumb-sized willow tree—and so did Dr. Vernon Bailey, another intrepid willow-hunter, just down from Parker Pass with a specimen of his own. No big-game trophy was ever sweeter to an Englishman on safari than was their double discovery of the snow willow to these two botanists.

Speaking of botany, it was in 1932 that the Harvey Monroe Hall Natural Area was established by the United States Forest Service in cooperation with the Carnegie Institution of Washington, D.C., just over the crest from Tioga Pass at the southeast foot of Mount Conness. The experimental station there, coordinating botanical research with sister stations at Mather and at Stanford University, has for many years contributed to heredity-environment studies.

Of course there were climbers. Although most Sierra peaks had long since been "conquered," others had remained inaccessible by then-current techniques.

The breakthrough came in the summer of 1931. Francis Farquhar had met Harvard philosopher and mathematician Robert Underhill, fresh from climbing in the Alps. Farquhar persuaded Underhill to join the Sierra Club Outing in the meadows to introduce European

*Park Ranger Naturalist Lowell Adams and a group
of hikers at Waterwheel Falls, 1938.*

climbing to the club. Under his tutelage, Farquhar led a small group directly up the face of Unicorn Peak, the first "properly roped" climb in the Sierra. Underhill then organized a regular climbing school and took his disciples to practice on the steep faces of Mount Ritter and Banner Peak, and to make a first ascent of Banner's east face. Later there was a "postgraduate course" on North Palisade and up the east face of Whitney.

Soon many climbers were re-exploring the Sierra with their new know-how. In 1932 the Sierra Club Rock Climbing Section was formed, giving great impetus to the sport.

The meadows bustled with activity, especially in the Budd Lake area where the air rang with piton hammerings and now and then a yodel of triumph. In 1931 Carl Sharsmith and Norman Clyde did a first ascent on the highest Echo Peak; Jules Eichorn, Glen Dawson, and Walter Brem on Matthes Crest; and Eichorn and Dawson on "Eichorn's Pinnacle" of Cathedral Peak.

From this beginning in Tuolumne Meadows, rock climbers spread out to attack hitherto unclimbed walls and faces up and down the range, notably in the Palisades and the Minarets, all of which were scaled before the decade was out.

Some climbers had a single first ascent to their credit; some, perhaps half a dozen. The man with more first ascents than any other American climber, the formidable mountain man of the Sierra, was Norman Clyde.

Clyde had finished college, done some work toward a master's degree in classical studies, and just after coming to the Sierra had suffered a devastating loss, the death of his young wife to tuberculosis. Not long after, he lost his last regular job, teaching at Bishop. Thereafter he lived alone, and mostly in the mountains. Others came for a season or many seasons. Norman came for all seasons. Others came for a few years; Norman, for a lifetime.

His ideas of gear were strange and imposing. For some fifty-five years he carried a legendary hundred-pound pack, out of which emerged the most bizarre objects: soft slippers for evening, four different cameras, and even a small library of books in French, German, and Latin.

It was not that he disliked people. On many a Sierra Club outing Clyde turned up to lead hikes and climbs, and those who climbed in the Sierra often sought him out to go with them. But most of all Norman loved the mountains, and when he had no companions, he

Tioga Road skirting Tenaya Lake, October 1935.

went alone. Some of his fabulous ascents were memorialized by nothing more than his name scrawled on an empty film box left on the summit.

One of the young climbers of that early wave in the '30s was Walter A. Starr, Jr., the original author of *Starr's Guide to the John Muir Trail and the High Sierra Region.* His fatal fall in the Minarets in 1933 is one of the never-to-be-forgotten tragedies of the Sierra, and Norman Clyde's discovery of his body after all others had given up, one of the remarkable searches.

In '34 the meadows even had a visiting potentate: Eleanor Roosevelt. This kindly and very urban lady arrived to announce she would take a trip into the back country. We can imagine the flurry of preparation as the rangers outfitted her for an expedition from Tuolumne Meadows to Young Lakes at the foot of Mount Conness.

Ranger Billy Nelson was in charge. He had already cut his teeth on celebrities when he told King Albert of Belgium, "You call me Billy and I'll call you King." History records that Nelson presented Mrs. Roosevelt with a hot water bottle to keep her feet warm. She offered to help with the cooking, but the crew politely declined—which was probably just as well, as she is known to have been innocent of such skills. The uppermost Young Lake has ever since been called Roosevelt Lake in her honor.

Thus were the meadows in season. But even the winter snows no longer sealed off the high country completely. In 1930 the first snow surveys were started as a joint venture of the National Park Service and the State of California, in order to estimate the amount of irrigation water that would be available each summer. Ranger C. C. Presnall has left us a description of the life of these crews:

"You stumble into camp by starlight, so leg weary that your muscles cramp when stooping to loosen the frozen ski harness. Your fingers are numb by the time a fire is started, but with plenty of hot tea and soup, you soon forget the cold. It is best also to forget that your wet socks have been hanging directly over the cooking soup. Remaining awake until the dishes are washed is a test of will power, but jumping out of your blankets into a zero atmosphere at three o'clock the next morning is an act of pure recklessness."

There was a day in late February, 1930 when four rangers headed up toward Tenaya Lake from Yosemite Valley. Out on the open granite in a whiteout of driving snow and gathering dusk, they lost their way.

Skier in Dana Meadows, with Mammoth Mountain in the background, 1933.

There was nothing for it but to start a fire, while they hollowed out a roofless igloo to cut the wind, and tried to sleep by hunching up on their Trapper Nelson packs. By daybreak the weather cleared and they plowed wearily through the deep snow until they reached the cabin at Tenaya Lake by mid-morning, had a big feed, and fell into bed for the rest of the day. Shades of Shelley Denton!

Nowadays snow measurements are made by automatic gauges, or by crews in mechanized vehicles. But romance is not completely dead, for teams still ski in several times a winter to check the equipment.

Not all high Yosemite skiing was business. In 1932 Dennis Jones and Milana Jank went from Mono Basin over Tioga Pass, through Tuolumne Meadows, and down to Yosemite Valley in thirty-six hours of skiing. Many have exuberantly followed the same trail since.

Then in March 1936 came the first winter ascent of Mount Lyell by Brower, Clark, Kaiser, Nilsson, and Robinson. On their second night out from the valley, holed into two mountain tents in a high wind, they concocted a gow of chocolate, cheese, and oatmeal, the altitude having evidently gone to their heads. The next day the wind was even fiercer. They had to take off their skis and crawl across the first spur of Mount Maclure. Hours later on the summit of Lyell, the wind died, and the view of an alpine Sierra, one great billowing snowy range, was the reward that only ski mountaineers can know.

Throughout the decade Ansel Adams had been traveling the high places and photographing their grandeur in ever more powerful visual statements. In 1930 he was made assistant manager of the Sierra Club outings. He is remembered from those days as a genial master of ceremonies at the evening campfires, and for his mock Greek tragedies such as King Dehydros of Exaustos, with a chorus of Weary Men and Sunburnt Women, and its sequel, The Trudgin' Women.

In a more serious vein, Adams wrote for the Sierra Club Bulletin, constantly stressing wilderness preservation. In 1936 the club sent Adams and his photographs to Washington to lobby for the establishment of a Kings Canyon National Park, which was finally signed into law in 1940. During the hearings, Adams spoke eloquently about the creation of a John Muir National Park stretching through all the high country from Yosemite south to Whitney. This glorious dream remains unrealized. Yet the inclusion of most of this region in wilderness areas does offer much of the protection which Adams envisioned. And the role of his great photographs of the Sierra in alerting the nation to the need to protect its natural beauty has been incalculable.

24

WAR AND PEACE

As the world plunged into the Second World War the mountains shone more gloriously beautiful than ever. Time, that had seemed as endless and promising as these great spaces, constricted and became precious. Sitting on the summit of Lyell, a climber who had just received his draft call might promise himself, "After it's over, I'll come back." To some, it would not be given to keep the promise.

Tuolumne Meadows became very quiet. Many were away in the service, or mobilized in war industries, and those who had the time were limited by gas rationing. Although the campground and Tuolumne Lodge were kept open, the park reduced its services. Sharsmith now tended an entrance station or worked on patrol in the valley. One summer he collected most of the material now in the Yosemite Herbarium. Meanwhile, Sierra skiers and climbers, now in the Mountain Troops, contributed their hard-won alpine know-how.

Then in time the distant storms subsided, the war did end. The lights, as the song said, went on again all over the world. How fresh and bright, how healing the mountains seemed to those returning! On Mount Dana, where few had climbed these many years, masses of sky pilot heralded peace, and the stubborn hope that is human blossomed in the meadows along with the shooting stars. Another generation discovered for itself the peace that passes understanding, the benison of the Sierra. For us as for each generation before us, the mountains were newly made and mint-bright, and unexplored because *we* had not explored them.

Trails were cleared, the campground once again echoed to the sounds of young families, and Carl Sharsmith was back leading hikes and climbs.

The '40s slipped into the '50s; the war receded, only to be replaced by the Cold War. Even in the mountains, the world was too much with us. By day, the huge blooming cumulus clouds Muir had so admired were criss-crossed by jet contrails, reminding us how close we were to everywhere else. On many an August night, lying in sleeping bags under the stars, our illusion of isolation was shattered when at dawn we would be awakened by a flash of light and later a distant boom: an atomic bomb test in the Nevada desert.

Thus was borne in upon us with a deeper awareness John Muir's observation, "Everything is hitched to everything else." There was no more frontier. No wilderness was inviolate, no solitude absolute.

Yet for campers, hikers and climbers, the '50s were a kind of golden age. It was possible then to walk the Muir Trail for a whole day and see only a few people. There were no fees and no time limits on your stay either in the meadows or the back country. You could leave your car at a trailhead for a month at a time and never give a thought to the chance of theft. You could build your fire in places where no one seemed ever to have camped before. As the Bushman said, speaking of his own idyllic past, "We were not poor then. We had all we could carry."

Halcyon days! Carl Sharsmith was no longer the only park naturalist in the meadows. There were Allan Waldo, genial geologist from the University of the Pacific; Will Neely, ceramic artist, wine connoisseur and botanist; and Allan Shields, philosophy professor and literary naturalist. They went just about everywhere in the Yosemite High Sierra, noting with pride that in a single summer they conducted fifty different all day hikes. Climbs, too, like Dana, Gibbs, Conness, Hoffmann, the Unicorn, Cathedral Peak, and Lyell. This last was an exciting three day trip, with the added luxury of a pack train carrying your gear to base camp.

In 1956 the National Park Service gave Sharsmith its meritorious service award for twenty-five years of outstanding work as a ranger naturalist. There was no hurry. Twenty-five years later he'd still be leading hikes.

For climbers, there were still some faces left unscaled, even out of Tuolumne Meadows. The north face and east ridge of Echo Ridge was climbed first by Firey, Hoessly, Hahn, and Robbins in 1949. Tarver

Photo courtesy of National Park Service. Photographer: Ralph Anderson.

Glen Aulin High Sierra Camp, 1948.

and Petrequin first ascended the northeast face of Cathedral Peak in 1953. And although the cutting edge of climbing had moved elsewhere, the peaks around the meadows still offered much challenge to the rope and piton contingent.

The '50s saw a great improvement in equipment. The nylon revolution made possible lighter, better gear. Vibram shoe soles appeared, and forever after humans left different tracks. Backpacks began to mutate and evolve, slowly at first, and later with the rapidity of fruit flies in a radiation laboratory. Dehydrated foods came on the market to lighten packs and simplify camp cuisine. The Dri-Lite Company advertised, "May your heart be as light as your Dri-Lite!"

This new and better equipment also facilitated ski touring. The winter solitude of the meadows was broken by more and more parties traversing the range on skis in the tracks of Jones and Jank. If they got into serious trouble there were helicopters to fly in and carry them to safety.

Up at the Sierra Club, Fred and Anne Eissler tended Parsons Lodge, living in the McCauley cabin with their two little girls. They came as soon as the road opened, and stayed until it closed, sometimes well into November. Fred and Anne had a deep commitment to the mountains and their preservation, and worked hard to spread the word. They posted neatly typed signs regarding wilderness dos and don'ts, especially on the inside of the outhouse doors, where you could not fail to read them.

The campground was animated with mountain-happy people. When it rained, what a pleasure to go up to Parsons Lodge for a quiet afternoon looking through bound issues of mountaineering journals, or going over maps to plan the next trip! By evening, a lodge campfire, and then back to camp over moonlit rocks, half-tempted to start right out and be on top of the peaks in time for sunrise. If it rained by dark, a few half-drowned backpackers muttering, "It never rains at night in the Sierra!" found their way to the lodge to sleep on a table and bless the sooty rafters and corrugated roof. But come morning: pancakes made light and bubbly with Soda Springs water . . . a white crowned sparrow nesting in the grasses . . . killdeer and other peeps announcing their ownership of the sunshine.

Yet as hikers returned from far and wide, they began to report that the back country was strewn with garbage dumps. Here was a painful meeting of old freedom and new reality. In the past hikers and more especially packers (who could bring in more stuff) habitually tossed cans, bottles, and old shoes into a dump near camp, serene in the thought that nature would rust it all back into earth. Now there were many more people with much more trash, and there were plastic and aluminum.

Something needed to be done, and Fred and Anne hatched the idea of the Cleanup Trip. The Sierra Club approved and offered to subsidize it. So for the first time in the summer of 1959, twenty volunteers spent a week cleaning out fireplaces, picking up bottles, smashing old cans, and bagging it all for packers to haul out. When the Cleanup Trip left an area, they posted signs exhorting others, "If you can pack it in full, you can pack it out empty." Now it's an old idea, and both the park service and the forest service have made packing out your trash a rule. Lower Lyell Base Camp, for example, is much cleaner because of this idea.

Halcyon days—yet things were changing. The park service became worried about its irreplaceable mountain meadows. Packers and hikers were streaming through these fragile areas, leaving deep ruts. So for a season in 1957 Carl Sharsmith did a study of meadow ecology. His report shocked the park service into action, and throughout the range they began restricting animal traffic and grazing, rerouting trails around, not through, meadows, and closing certain over-traveled areas to camping. In the Tuolumne Meadows area the trails to Glen Aulin and up the Lyell Fork were partially rerouted through the woods.

Then too, something was happening to the trees. Although the meadows region also has mountain hemlocks, junipers, western white and Jeffrey pines, red fir, and whitebark pine—nevertheless, by far most of the trees are lodgepole pines. Not so graceful as the hemlock, nor so colorful as the juniper, nor so stately as the fir, in dense forests the lodgepole is monotonous. But when it stands alone at meadow-edge or on a windswept ridge, its rugged silhouette has a singular beauty. Around the Tuolumne Meadows and flanking the surrounding mountains, lodgepoles grow in thick stands, and like a mono-culture in farming, their very success makes them especially vulnerable to their enemies. The greatest of these is the needleminer moth.

These tiny gray creatures flutter out of the trees in July and fill the air for a few weeks. When they lay their eggs, the larvae that emerge are minute pink worms. Each one bores into a lodgepole needle. A single larva will eat out a needle, then migrate to another, about four times a season. Then every other year (and mysteriously, all in the same year) they eat their way out and fly as moths.

By late July of their flight year the dead needles have fallen and new growth takes their place. But when winters are mild the needleminer population increases, and as it builds up over several years they begin to threaten the forest. Three successive infestations (six years) will so weaken the trees that bark beetles and other enemies can finish them off.

By 1947 the needleminers were approaching epidemic proportions in the Tenaya Lake area and in Tuolumne Meadows. The park service was alarmed. That summer they sprayed the forest with DDT, the new miracle insecticide. In 1953, 11,000 acres of the area were again sprayed with DDT. Maybe that would fix the pesky bugs! It didn't, and a few people began to wonder if that was the way.

The isolation of Tuolumne Meadows was almost at an end. The Twenty-one Mile Stretch of the Tioga Road grew more notorious as the population swelled. After much controversy, the park service decided to reroute and modernize the stretch. In the summer of 1957, Sharsmith returned from leading a Mount Lyell climb and noticed with a sorry heart the heavy equipment moving in. It is ironic that the new road was being started at the very moment in history when keener foresight might have suggested *reducing* impact in the interest of preservation.

Ansel Adams was also concerned. In 1958 on a hike to Tenaya Lake, he was outraged at the desecration of the area, particularly of the rounded bosses of superb glacial polish which were being blasted. Although the work was well along, he contacted the interior secretary, the commerce secretary, and the National Park Service director, who ordered a temporary halt in construction for an investigation. Adams wrote, "A blemish on the face of Venus is a serious matter, beyond the proportion of the area it occupies!"

But the fat was in the fire. Not even Ansel Adams could save Tenaya's shore, while in the meadows, great gobs of sand were being shoveled out of the Tuolumne River bed for road construction. This would leave a strange unnatural depression, flooding in early summer and ragged and raw later, where once the mountain stream had meandered among willows and flowery meadows. Venus had acquired several blemishes, and another golden age was drawing to a close.

25

THE TURBULENT SIXTIES AND SEVENTIES

Then the '60s were upon us. As the decade began, no one could foresee the changes it would bring to America, to Yosemite—even to Tuolumne Meadows.

In 1961 the new section of the Tioga Road opened with great hoopla. An enthusiastic public crowded in to admire the newly-accessible views, the generous parking areas, and the neat metal signs indicating natural features. Few mourned the old Twenty-one Mile Stretch. Predictably, the meadows campground was crowded that year. Old-timers in the habit of staying all season were told their time was limited and they must move on. For some, it was like being turned out of the old homestead.

In 1962 Lee and Dorothy Verret became custodians at the Sierra Club Campground. They had come to Yosemite from Louisiana in 1921 as newlyweds, and spent the summer of 1925 at the Soda Springs. Later Lee worked as a forest ranger and park ranger. Now they took over Parsons Lodge and stayed every summer through 1971, longer than any other custodians. Lee, an able carpenter, reroofed the McCauley cabin and made many needed repairs.

Looking back on those years, the Veretts recalled meeting many mountaineers to whom Tuolumne Meadows was a special kind of home. Among them was Norman Clyde, an old man now, yet still with a huge pack and an appetite to match. He and others, revisiting the scenes of their youth, came to drink a sacramental cup of soda water and talk about the old days.

In the summer of 1970 the Verrets celebrated their golden wedding anniversary at the lodge, complete with champagne (compliments of Curry Company) and many loyal friends to honor the day. Seven years later, a simple gathering in front of the lodge held a memorial service for Lee. Ranger Ferdinand Castillo read a moving tribute to his friend who had known and loved this place for over fifty years.

Herb Ewing, son and grandson of Yosemite rangers, became chief ranger of the Mather District, which included Tuolumne Meadows, and continued for many years administrating this mountain domain. Another familiar face in the meadows: Nic Fiori, popular head of the Yosemite Ski School in winter, and in summer manager of the High Sierra Camps. Ferdinand Castillo began his long tenure at Tioga Pass entrance station. Those who come or leave that way know well his cheery greeting, his fund of information, and his passionate defense of every blade of grass in his high realm.

Meanwhile construction proceeded on the road between Tioga Pass and Lee Vining, twelve miles east and 3,000 feet down. This was the dizzying stretch that had terrified Mather's party in 1916. Though it had been improved from time to time, it still gave the jim-jams to flatlanders, and deterred many from driving through the park. Opened in 1964, the new road is a marvel of engineering which achieves the descent in one vast sweep without a single switchback.

Now indeed all was different. Although commercial trucking was prohibited through the park, all manner of thirty-foot trailers and motor homes could easily get to the meadows. Many of these new visitors saw the mountains as a park in the conventional sense, a recreational area, rather than as a wilderness. The meadows sprouted with such hitherto unfamiliar gear as volley and beach balls, baseball bats, air mattresses to float on the river and rafts to run it, and frisbees. The staccato barking of motor scooters as well as the blaring of radios and tapes often drowned out chattering chickarees and hammering woodpeckers. Happily, in time many of these newcomers became converts to wilderness values and joined the hiking-fishing-climbing fraternity, thereby enriching their lives. However, the ranger naturalists (now called interpreters) found fewer takers for their most strenuous hikes and climbs. Mount Conness was dropped, Pothole Dome maintained.

Another sizable group of visitors represented what was called the New Lifestyle. Kerouac had anticipated them back in the '50s when he

Bennettville today, with Mount Dana in the background.

made it to North Yosemite and climbed Matterhorn Peak on brown rice and swigs of cheap port.

With the Vietnam War, campus unrest, the Civil Rights and Free Speech movements, and sometimes drugs, the scene changed profoundly. A generation gap as deep as the Tuolumne Canyon appeared. Young people came to the meadows in funky clothes, sitting crosslegged on the ground and speaking a stylized slang that set them apart. Emerson's injunction to "do your thing" became their rallying cry. Nudism was in vogue when mosquitoes weren't too bad.

Yet much of their revolt was more inward. Buddhism and other exotic religions were searched out for what they could teach. Large numbers began to turn to nature as to something clean and good and kindly in a world gone sour. It was not unusual to see a group in the full lotus position in the meadows, meditating among the ivesia and pussy toes. What better place to seek for truth on a bright dewy morning?

There was a great increase in backpacking—but what backpacking! With little mountain know-how, they plunged across the landscape. Barefoot on granite, tentless under storms, starved, soaked, blistered, and frequently stoned, they fouled their drinking water and fell off rocks. Unknowingly they mistreated the very wilderness they loved. The so-fragile mountain flora was threatened by botanical innocents trying to live off the country, who plundered the edible and the poisonous alike to concoct their herbal teas.

Of course these exaggerated cases were a minority. There were also, as ever, knowledgeable backpackers and respecters of wilderness hitting the high passes. But there were so many! Running the campground grew more difficult. The same was true of the Sierra Club Campground at the Soda Springs, where many non-members invaded the place, ignoring the long-established rules. To some visitors the rangers seemed to represent the suspect Establishment with their regulations, short hair, and trim uniforms. Most of them committed the sin of being over thirty!

In response to changing times, security forces in the park were beefed up. Concommittantly an effort was made to hire younger personnel who would be able to relate to and communicate with their own generation. For the first time we saw rangers who wore beards and talked cool.

By 1972 the interpretive program was greatly broadened to appeal to a wider gamut of interests with, for example, star walks, sunset meditations, night prowls, night-long moon-eclipse watches, and seminars in rock climbing and backpacking.

Another movement, Women's Liberation, finally breached the sex barrier. The park service, long a bastion of masculinity, brought in many women. During the first few years there were jokes about "rangerettes." But the women soon showed by their ability and devotion that they could hold their own. The National Park Service learned what Parsons had discovered seventy years before, and gradually women came to share all kinds of duties on an equal basis with the men.

Rock climbing and mountain survival generated so much interest that the concessioners opened a mountaineering school in the meadows which supplemented park service offerings in these areas. They also opened a mountain shop. Climbing techniques were changing. There was more emphasis on free climbing using rope and hardware for security, rather than direct aid. Lembert, Murphy's, and Polly domes became training faces for neophyte rock climbers, festooned with vari-colored ropes. Legions of tee shirts advised, "Go Climb a Rock."

People-management was not the only problem confronting the park service. By the '70s the crime rate among bears was soaring. Car windows were shattered, tents slashed, iceboxes smashed, and sleeping bags ripped. A night spent anywhere along the Lyell Fork was apt to produce a Bear Incident, with the hiker usually the loser. Although the animals usually did not harm people, their toll of expensive camping gear was appalling.

How to retrain the bruins to go back to the woods where they belonged? For a long time, marauding bears had been trapped and deported to remote areas of the park. Now a massive campaign was begun to retrain the people. It became a legal offense to leave food where bears might find it. Then Yosemite developed its gift to the world: a real bear-proof garbage bin. The bears soon learned to leave the bins alone. Gradually the most incorrigible animals were eliminated or died off, and the bear menace, though not obliterated, was greatly reduced.

There were still the needleminers. In 1955 a summer field camp of entomologists had started a ten year study of the insect in Tuolumne Meadows. A prime objective was to discover its native enemies as a potential control—while the park service continued to spray, now with malathion. Before the study was completed, Dr. Alan D. Telford became confident that the needleminer's enemies were on the increase, but he worried that the malathion would kill them too, and thus *increase* the infestation.

Then in 1962 Rachel Carson's *Silent Spring* was published. Although Carson may never have come to Tuolumne Meadows, her message did. This landmark book would bring home to the world the devastating effect of pesticides. By 1963 Fred Eissler published an article voicing vigorous Sierra Club opposition to the spraying. The club did not allow it on the Soda Springs property.

By the late '70s the needleminer didn't seem quite so threatening any more, and spraying was discontinued. Years of study and thought had resulted in a new way of looking at the insects. They were part of the scene. An important, perhaps an essential part.

As it preys on the lodgepole pine, the needleminer periodically kills off stands of mature trees—and thus opens up the forest and allows new growth. Over hundreds of years, individual trees sicken and die, but the forest remains healthy. Then too, a thick forest absorbs more moisture than a thinned-out one. If most of the moisture were bound in the trees, there would be little to flow down and form a sponge in the glacial basin—a sponge where no trees could grow. Could it be partly the needleminer which we have to thank for Tuolumne Meadows?

The existence of a Sierra Club enclave at the Soda Springs began to seem something of an anomaly. After the Second World War the park service became more dedicated to buying up inholdings in all national parks, and the Sierra Club encouraged it to do so. Finally in 1973 Yosemite received funds from the new Land and Water Conservation Act to purchase the property.

So, in an era of many beginnings and endings, thus ended another tradition as the Sierra Club terminated its historic presence in Tuolumne Meadows.

Before the transfer, the club had eliminated car traffic in order to reduce campground erosion. Now for three years the park service operated it as a walk-in campground with a ranger living at the McCauley cabin. Parsons Lodge remained open part of the time, and continued to serve as a source of information and inspiration to park visitors.

However, the increasing impact on the meadows concerned the park service. So in 1976 they removed the tables and dismantled the old fireplaces. The Soda Springs campground, where lovers of the high places had gathered for more than seventy-five years, was no more. All that remain are ghosts of those who came before and left this legacy of mountains and sky. Perhaps most poignant of all, the Edward Taylor Parsons Memorial Lodge was shuttered and padlocked, fallen into disuse.

Fortunately its history does not end there. The lodge has been declared a National Historic Site. Since that time, the Yosemite Natural History Association has reopened it each summer. Once again it has become a reading room where visitors can enjoy books and magazines on nature and conservation. And associated with the lodge, classes open to the public take off with YNHA naturalists like Michael Ross to study the many-faceted mountain world. This beautiful building remains a symbol of the inception of the conservation movement in California, and of the Sierra Club, its spearhead for so many decades.

Meadows, like people, do not stand still, but wear and age. And people have accelerated the process. In areas where sheepherding was heaviest the soil was compacted and the water table lowered, allowing trees to encroach upon meadows which had formerly been too wet for them. Furthermore, when the paved Tioga Road was put in along the southern edge of Tuolumne Meadows in 1938, the road acted as a dike and prevented some of the runoff from the north-facing mountain slopes from seeping through. This too made the meadows drier and allowed tree invasion. Being partly responsible for this ecological change, the park service regularly cuts down small trees which spring up along the meadow rim by the road, and which would eventually obscure the view if left to grow.

Below the Soda Springs on a hot August day in 1985, Superintendent Robert Binneweis and the Adams family brought together an illustrious group to name and dedicate Mount Ansel Adams, a peak the famous photographer had loved and frequently climbed during his lifetime. They also dedicated Yosemite as a World Heritage Site, further honoring its place in the hearts of the entire world. Among others, Director of the National Park Service William Penn Mott, Secretary of the Interior Donald Hodel, conservationist and Sierran David Brower, writer Wallace Stegner, and actor Robert Redford all spoke movingly of the beauties of nature which Adams had celebrated in his pictures and writings, and the need to be ever vigilant in their protection.

Part of the change has been in the natural order of things. The past thirty or forty years have been uncommonly warm, as Sierra weather goes. When it warms, all meadows become drier, and the rimming lodgepole pines begin to close in. You can see this today in Tuolumne Meadows, even far from the road, and elsewhere up and down the Sierra. If the trend continues, these lovely flowery basins will surrender to the devouring forest—at least for a while. Later there may be another shift toward colder and wetter conditions, the forest may move back again, and the meadows be reborn. Some day.

Seasons change and so do people. Perhaps one of the most gently changed of all has been Carl Sharsmith. Over the years he has been transmuted from the young preacher of wilderness values to the sage of Tuolumne Meadows. In the '70s he and others began leading alpine seminars for the Yosemite Natual History Association. Carl reinstituted the glacier measurements which Matthes had begun. Thereafter through the summer of 1983 (as of this writing) he has taught alpine and subalpine botany, and continued his work as a ranger naturalist as well.

He still has that jaunty Stetson bought in 1926. Now all the seams have been restitched by hand, and though no self-respecting moth would consider it, it suits him better than ever. His fifty-year-old flashlight, his 1935 Ford roadster, his handmade plant press—all bespeak the lifelong Swiss frugality which has become a legend. Legendary, too, are his kindness, humor, and generosity of spirit. Above all, he still draws strength and joy from the mountains as an old pine draws nutrients from the soil.

Twenty-five years after his first award, the park service gave him another, the First Yosemite Award, for fifty years of meritorious service. But then, for Carl as for A. E. Housman,

> "to look at things in bloom,
> fifty springs are little room."

26

TODAY AND TOMORROW

As we look around in the '80s, we see Tuolumne Meadows as something of a paradox.

White men have been here for almost a hundred and fifty years; Indians, for untold centuries. The Indians, as Muir remarked, left little to show for their long occupation. Their successors have dealt less lightly. And now the old expansive freedoms have been chipped away. Permits and limitations on back country travel, no fires above 9,600 feet, no camping within 100 feet of streams and lakes, only two weeks a year to stay in the automobile campground: rules and regulations on every side. A managed wilderness, a paradox indeed!

Yet all this management is in order to keep the high country a place of beauty where man can still go to renew his relationship with nature. While automobiles roar through on the road, only a few steps away you can be alone with the mountains in the finest, most purifying sense.

In a few ways it is less managed than formerly. Not so many fish are planted as in the past, although they are planted frequently in the Inyo National Forest just east of Tioga Pass. We don't spray the needleminer, or put out lightning-ignited fires, for we realize now that fire and needleminers both help to keep the forest healthy.

The outside world brings its own changes to the meadows. For a while it seemed that huge RV's would turn the campground into a parking lot for monsters. But with soaring gasoline prices, there has been a return to small cars. Almost overnight the campground sprouted anew with nylon tents of rainbow colors and wondrously complex architecture. It looked like a campground again. Some arrivals have abandoned cars altogether in favor of ten-speed bikes, motorcycles, and thumbs.

More visitors from other countries are finding their way here, and we hear German and French, Spanish and Japanese along the trails. They are getting to know us and our mountains, just as many Americans have come to know theirs.

Popular as the national parks are with Americans and others, financing them has always been touch-and-go. Each year Congress funds the parks anew. Some years it delays until late in the session, and the park service has to cinch up its belt and reduce staff or services. Considering their all too-frequent bare-bones funding through the years, one can only admire the dedication of the park service people in taking care of our parks for us. We owe them a debt of thanks, and all the support and help we can give.

For years now the park service has been working on a General Management Plan for Yosemite. After input by experts and laymen and many public meetings and discussions, it was finally adopted in 1980.

For Tuolumne Meadows the plan foresees a number of changes: improving employee housing, relocating a few buildings and the stables, upgrading the sewer system, removing some nonessential roads. Already the campground has been reduced to 320 sites, and many of the loveliest sites along the river and along Unicorn Creek have been taken out as a means of reducing water pollution. The finest old landmarks—Parsons Lodge, the McCauley Cabin, Soda Springs enclosure, and the old CCC Visitors' Center—will stay to add their mellow reminder of days gone by.

Meanwhile, interpreters continue to walk the trails and show newcomers their wonders, and old-timers can return again and again with joy and appreciation ever-new to Tuolumne Meadows. Thus, in a world in flux, the park service continues to try to fulfill its difficult double mandate to preserve the natural environment, and yet provide for its use and enjoyment by the people.

When you have been around as long as Carl Sharsmith, you take the long view. One day he was gazing thoughtfully at that ever-fascinating rim of mountains, that ever-charming carpet of grasses. "What are you thinking about, Carl?" asked a companion.

"I was thinking about what the meadows would be a hundred years from now," he replied. "Probably much the same as now. I hope so."

So do we all!

Upper Lyell Base Camp, with Dave Brower and a Paramount movie crew, 1936. Mount Lyell can be seen in the background.

27

REFLECTIONS BY THE RIVER: THERE IS STILL A MEADOW

We have lingered late this year, and September is almost gone. Early storms have already whitened the high peaks and melted off again, except for a few patches. Now the sky is deep blue, the air still, the meadows brown. In the grasses, Newberry's gentian and Yosemite aster go on blooming. Along the river the sedges are trampled down by summer walkers, a few of whom wander still in the hushed moment before winter. The river is so low you can walk across it on stones.

Yes, there is still a meadow. Lembert Dome shines, and a few figures are silhouetted against the sky on top. Mount Dana and Mount Gibbs, the purple twins of the eastern escarpment, stand dreaming in the sun, serene as old men. Cathedral Peak has never seemed sharper, or the Unicorn more jaunty, or Fairview Dome rounder, or the world lovelier.

They are gone now: Lembert and Brewer, Le Conte and Muir, Parsons and Colby, Norman Clyde, and the others. They walked this way once, and loved it as we have loved it, and then they went away. But the meadow remains.

It, too, is not eternal. It too came, changed, is changing now, and will in time be no more. But its time is longer, so much longer than a man's time.

And what we must consider—we who come briefly and pass quickly—is what we do to this meadow which is greater and longer-lived than ourselves.

We cannot now relate to wilderness as merely visitors who enjoy, abuse, and then pass on. It is not a free and wild frontier. It is simply part of our home. As much our home as the foundering polluted cities, the neat sterile suburbs, the chemistry-ridden farmlands, or the sea which can no longer engulf all man's mistakes and remain pure. They are all our home, and we must be stewards to them all—for we haven't anything else.

And if we fail the mountains, we will fail the sea and the valleys and the cities too. And ultimately, ourselves.

There are those who find some conflict between the values of wilderness and the values of man. Nothing could be blinder. Yet not all human beings have been so blind.

It has been observed that western civilization long ago went astray and started down a trail that seemed at first to offer promise and hope, but will finally end in disaster. The error was in that feeling of omnipotence when mankind seemed to say, "I am not the creature of my mother, the earth, and I need not obey her rules. The earth and all upon it were placed here for my convenience, and I need only be strong enough, and clever enough, and I will conquer all her secrets and eat all her fruits."

How the old-time American Indians would have laughed at that—they who knew that the Salmon People and the Bear People and the Deer People exist equally with the Human People in loving interdependence, and all need each other.

How the ancient Hindus would have laughed at that—they who knew that the mountains are themselves divinities, and that the life and consciousness of a man or woman proceeds through this God-imbued universe interchangeably expressed in bird or beast or flower or human form, forever seeking that divine union with everything, which will end the search.

How Saint Francis would have laughed, as he sang to Brother Sun and Sister Moon, and fed the wild wolf and preached to the birds.

And now that western man has pushed his kind of reality almost to the limits, and finds dominion eluding him and the fruits escaping his grasp—now he must look to these other realities, these other kinds of human wisdom, for what they can teach him.

They are all metaphors for something fundamental which we must win back to: that we live on the earth within the limits which earth, not man, sets. If we waste and poison the water, we will die, for we must have good water. If we pollute the air we will die, for we depend upon air. If we continue to increase our populations we will die, for earth can only support so many of us. And if we perfect and use our war machines, we will surely die.

The mountains, of course, will remain. They will change, but they will not be destroyed. Yet to human beings contemplating their own possible self-extinction, that is perhaps cold comfort.

But there is still hope. We must consider carefully everything we do now. The earth which has tolerated man and tried to forgive his errors, now depends upon him, and he cannot make too many more mistakes. As the needleminer cannot quite destroy the forest, or it will destroy itself, we must also limit our destructiveness. As the Clark's nutcracker cannot devour all the pinenuts in the forest, or there would be no forest, we too must curb our greed. As the lichens creep over rock fractures and the grasses over unused trails, we must heal and mend and grow again, for that is the way of things if they are to go on.

We must preserve our mountains, our meadows, our wilderness areas, not just because it is nice to take walks in the woods, although it is. We must preserve them for all mankind as sources of pure water, as forests to cleanse the air, as reservoirs of our brothers and sisters, the animals and birds and insects and plants whose importance we may not yet have discovered. And above all, as places where human beings can find again that harmonious relation with nature, that Right Way as the Buddhists would have it, upon which their very life depends.

So I close this book about the past, with some hope for the future. As long as we have the meadow, there is much left that is good in our world. May we cherish the meadow for those who will yet come with open souls and youthful hearts, as to a world newborn, and who will find peace and joy and happiness there, and perhaps wisdom. It is not too much to hope.

Newberry's Gentian *(Gentiana newberryi)*

CHRONOLOGY

Before the Arrival of White Men

28,000 to 20,000 B.C.   Firm evidence of man in the New World.
c. 7,000 B.C.   People are first found crossing the Sierra.
1300s to 1800s A.D.   Little Ice Age.

Nineteenth Century

1833   Joseph Reddeford Walker crosses the Sierra, taking the ridge
       between the Tuolumne and Merced watersheds, but missing
       Tuolumne Meadows.
1851   Savage's Battalion enters Yosemite Valley.
       March 25, Chief Tenaya and part of his tribe captured.
       May 22, Boling captures the Indians at Lake Tenaya.
1857   There is a rush of miners from the town of Tuolumne, over the
       Mono Trail, to Mono Diggings.
       Tom McGee of Big Oak Flat probably blazes the Mono Trail.
       The "Great Circle Route" is started by sheepherders.
1860   Doc Chase stakes his claim on Tioga Hill.
       The California State Geological Survey established, with Profes-
       sor Josiah Dwight Whitney in charge.
1863   The geological survey visits Tuolumne Meadows.
1864   Brewer and Frederick Law Olmstead visit Tuolumne Meadows
       and make first ascent of Mount Gibbs, on horseback.
       Yosemite State Park established by President Lincoln.
1869   John Muir's first summer in the Sierra, and his first ascent of Ca-
       thedral Peak.
1870   Joseph LeConte and the University Excursion Party visit Tuo-
       lumne Meadows.

1871   Muir goes down the Grand Canyon of the Tuolumne.
        Muir publishes "The Death of a Glacier."
1872   William Keith's first visit to Tuolumne Meadows.
1873   Muir revisits Tuolumne Canyon with Keith, Kellogg, and Mrs.
            Carr.
1875   Brusky finds Doc Chase's old claim, and takes ore sample.
1876   Brusky takes more and better samples.
        Muir's first essay on sheep devastation of the Sierra.
1878   Mining rush begins in Tioga Mining District.
        John L. Murphy settles at Tenaya Lake.
        High Sierra surveyed by Macomb of the Wheeler Survey. Macomb
            climbs Mount Lyell.
1879   Davidson on Mount Conness for the United States Coast
            and Geodetic Survey.
1880   Shelley Denton goes through Tuolumne Meadows.
        Dana City has a post office.
1881   Great Sierra Consolidated Silver Company commences work at
            the Great Sierra Mine.
        Silver found on Mount Hoffmann, and Mount Hoffmann Mining
            District is established, but comes to nothing.
1882   Construction of the Tioga Road is started.
1882-83 Israel Russell and survey party in Tuolumne Meadows for the
            summer.
        Willard Johnson goes down the Lyell bergschrund.
1883   Tioga Road completed.
1884   Great Sierra Mine closed.
        Theodore Solomons gets the idea for the John Muir Trail.
1885   Lembert takes up a claim at Soda Springs.
1886   John L. Murphy preempts 160 acres at Tenaya Lake.
1887   Davidson is back on Mount Conness.
1889   Muir and Johnson come to Tuolumne Meadows, and decide to
            push for the establishment of Yosemite National Park.
1890   October 1, Yosemite National Park established.
        Davidson is back on Mount Conness, surveying.
1891   Captain Wood becomes the first acting superintendent of park.
1892   May 28, Sierra Club charter signed.
1893   First Sierra Club Bulletin.
1894   William Colby's first trip to Tuolumne Meadows.
1896   John Lembert is murdered.
1898   Spanish-American War; troops are temporarily withdrawn from
            park, and Archie Leonard is made first civilian ranger.
        The McCauleys buy the Soda Springs property.

Twentieth Century

1901 First Sierra Club Outing to Tuolumne Meadows.
Death of Professor Joseph LeConte.

1905 The park boundary is reduced, and the Ritter Range and Devil's
Postpile are removed from the park.
François Matthes starts his survey of Yosemite Valley.

1906 Recession of Yosemite Valley to the government; it becomes part
of Yosemite National Park.

1907 Sierra Club Outing to Hetch Hetchy.

1911 Tenaya Lake trail from Yosemite Valley completed.

1912 Sierra Club buys the Soda Springs property.

1913 December 17, the Raker Bill passes, and Hetch Hetchy is lost.
First Bureau of National Parks formed.

1914 Death of John Muir and Edward Parsons
Museum of Vertebrate Zoology of the University of California
begins five year field study of the animal life of Yosemite.
The army leaves and civilian administrators take over.
Stephen Mather becomes head of the National Park Service, and
buys the Tioga Road.

1915 Parsons Lodge built by the Sierra Club.
First appropriation by the State of California for the John Muir
Trail.
Discovery of the Mount Lyell salamander by the University of
California Survey.

1916 Stephen Mather made director of National Park Service and brings
a party of important men to Tuolumne Meadows.
Tuolumne Meadows Lodge and Tenaya Camp opened.

1918 High Sierra Camps closed because of bankruptcy of the company.

1921 Holdup and robbery at Lake Tenaya.

1923 High Sierra Hikers' Camps reopened.

1924 Hoof and mouth disease epidemic among Yosemite deer; large
numbers of deer destroyed.
Publication of *Animal Life in the Yosemite* by Grinnell and
Storer.
Glen Aulin and Vogelsang High Sierra camps opened.

1925 **Yosemite School of Field Natural History organized.**

1929 **Orland Bartholomew arrives in Tuolumne Meadows after traveling on skis the length of the Sierra from Cottonwood Canyon in
winter.**

1930 High Sierra Snow Surveys organized by National Park Service and
State of California.

Publication of Matthes's *Geologic History of Yosemite.*

Carl Sharsmith enters the Yosemite Field School.

1931 Glacier measurements instituted by Matthes in the Yosemite High Sierra.

Underhill, Farquhar et al. introduce modern rope management in climbing on the north face of the Unicorn.

Carl Sharsmith becomes the first ranger naturalist at Tuolumne Meadows.

A Sierra Club trip goes down the Grand Canyon of the Tuolumne and returns by Matterhorn Canyon to Soda Springs.

1932 Sierra Club Rock Climbing Section organized.

Harvey Monroe Hall Natural Area established.

Dennis Jones and Milana Jank cross the Sierra on skis from Mono Basin to Yosemite Valley.

1933 Civilian Conservation Corps comes to Yosemite.

Salix nivalis discovered on Mount Dana and Koip Pass.

Walter A. Starr, Jr., author of *Starr's Guide to the John Muir Trail,* lost in the Minarets.

1934 Eleanor Roosevelt visits Young Lakes.

1935 Carl Sharsmith falls off the top of Mount McClure and is rescued.

1936 New campground opened in Tuolumne Meadows with 300 sites.

Ansel Adams is sent to Washington by the Sierra Club to lobby.

1938 Tenaya Lake High Sierra Camp is removed and a new camp established at May Lake.

Tuolumne Meadows Visitors' Center is built by the CCC.

Tioga Road is partially paved and rerouted along the south side of Tuolumne Meadows.

Publication of *Sierra Nevada: The John Muir Trail* by Ansel Adams.

1940 Tioga Road is rebuilt "on modern standards."

1942 CCC leaves Yosemite.

1943 Ranger naturalist program discontinued as a war measure.

1947 Heavy infestation of lodgepole pine needleminer in Tenaya Lake and Tuolumne Meadows region.

1948 Very dry year. Worst fire in park history, in Pate Valley; Tuolumne Meadows staff sent to fight the fire.

François Matthes receives gold medal from the Department of the Interior for fifty-one years of meritorious service.

Yosemite Field School resumes after lapse during World War II.

Annual glacier surveys are resumed.

1949 First use of helicopter for rescue in Yosemite: an injured boy is brought out from Benson Lake area.

1951 Yosemite Centennial.

First airplane planting of trout in Yosemite.

1952 Heaviest winter since 1911, with twice the normal snowfall.

1953 Worst fire season in park records.

   First large scale control effort for lodgepole pine needleminer: 11,000 acres of the 45,000 infested are sprayed with DDT from airplanes.

   Yosemite Field School suspended.

1955 Ten year study of needleminers started in Tuolumne Meadows.

1956 Carl Sharsmith receives National Park Service Meritorious Service Award for twenty-five years of service.

1957 New Tioga Road started.

1958 Helicopter used in needleminer control work, Tuolumne Meadows.

   Ansel Adams temporarily halts construction of the Tioga Road, but it is later resumed.

1959 First Sierra Club Cleanup Trip, in southern Sierra.

1961 Dedication of final park section of new Tioga Road.

   Sunrise High Sierra Camp opened.

1962 Publication of Rachel Carson's *Silent Spring.*

   Lee and Dorothy Verret become custodians at Soda Springs.

1963 Work begun on modernization of Tioga Road from Tioga Pass to Lee Vining.

   Publication of *The Natural History of the Sierra Nevada* by Tracy Storer and Robert Usinger.

   Sierra Club opposes spraying of needleminer in Tuolumne Meadows.

1964 Opening of rebuilt Tioga Road from Tioga Pass to Lee Vining.

1967 Yosemite receives greatest snowpack to date; Tioga Road not opened until June 17.

1969 Another record breaking snowfall.

1971 Prescribed burning begun in Yosemite.

1972 Interpretive activities greatly broadened to meet the needs of the new generation of visitors.

1973 Music Corporation of America buys Yosemite Park and Curry Company.

   Park service buys the Sierra Club's Soda Springs property and Parsons Lodge.

1976 Walk-in campground at Soda Springs closed.

1980 Old Visitors' Center in Tuolumne Meadows closed; center moved to the old CCC mess hall.

1981 Carl Sharsmith receives the National Park Service award for fifty years of meritorious service.

1982-83 Two winters of extremely heavy snowfall. Tioga Pass not opened until July 4, 1983.

CHRONOLOGY OF SOME FIRST ASCENTS IN THE TUOLUMNE MEADOWS REGION

1863	Mount Dana, Fairview Dome, Ragged Peak	Brewer and Hoffman
	Mount Hoffman	Whitney, Brewer and Hoffman
1864	Mount Gibbs (on horseback)	Brewer and Olmsted
1866	Mount Conness	King and Gardiner
1868	Mount Warren	Wackenreyder
1869	Cathedral Peak	Muir
1870	Tower Peak	Hoffman, Goodyear, and Craven
1870s	Rodgers Peak	Muir, probably
1871	Mount Lyell	Tileston
1872	Mount Ritter	Muir
1878	Dunderberg Peak	Macomb and Wheeler Survey
1883	Mount McClure	Johnson
	Banner Peak	Johnson and Miller
1891	Mount Davis	Davis
1892	Mount Lyell (first women)	Gompertz and Miller
1895	Donohue Peak (on horse-back)	Donohue
1896	Polly Dome	Solomons and four girls
1897	Mount Florence	Solomons and Reed
1899	Matterhorn Peak	Dempster, Hutchinson, Hutchinson and Noble
1902	Mammoth Peak	Huber
1909	Kuna Crest	Huber
1911	Unicorn, northeast face	Farquhar and Rennie
1912	Koip Peak	Versteeg
1914	Parker Peak	Clyde
	Electra Peak	Clyde
	Foerster Peak	Clyde
	Cockscomb	Lipman and Chamberlain
1917	White Mountain	Huber

1919	Kuna Peak	Huber
1921	Columbia Finger	Staniels, Tripp, and Bochner
1923	(or earlier) Vogelsang Peak	Matthes
1931	Highest Echo Peak	Sharsmith and Clyde
	Matthes Crest	Eichorn, Dawson, and Brem
	Simmons Peak	Sierra Club members
	Excelsior Mountain	Sloan
1933	Shepherd Crest	Blanks, May, and Sawyer
	Johnson Peak	Blanks
	Volcanic Ridge	Barbash and Gates
1934	Sheep Peak	May and Twining
1936	Mount Lyell (first ski ascent)	Robinson, Brower, Clark, Kaiser and Nilsson
1937	North Peak	Blanchard, North, and Leech
1949	Echo Ridge, north face and east ridge	Firey, Hoessly, Hahn, and Robbins
no date	Rafferty Peak	Hernden

No Record of First Ascents

Mount Lewis	Blacktop Peak	Fletcher Peak
Mount Wood	Tenaya Peak	Tuolumne Peak
Tioga Peak	Lee Vining Peak	Lembert Dome

GLOSSARY

accipiter   one of several woodland hawks with short, broad wings and a long tail; e.g., Cooper's hawk

alidade   a topographic surveying and mapping instrument

anther   the pollen-bearing tip of the stamen or male part of a flower

assay   chemical analysis of a rock sample to ascertain the amount of metal in it

basalt   a hard dense dark volcanic rock formed by lava flowing above ground

batholith   a large formation of igneous rock that has intruded into other layers of rock at great depths under the earth

bergschrund   a crevasse at the head of a glacier where the moving ice has broken away from the rock wall above

cache   a store of hidden goods; in the Sierra, often a can containing supplies which a backpacker can pick up part way through his trip

chaparral   dense thicket of shrubs and small trees characteristic of the California foothills; its roots are not destroyed by fire, and its seeds germinate best in the wake of one.

chatter mark   a short, usually crescent shaped crack in a boulder or on bedrock at right angles to the line of glacial scratches showing where the glacier moved a small stone sporadically across the surface

cleavage joints   joints or cracks in rock, formed along parallel lines due to the internal structure of the rock

contrail   condensation trail of water vapor or ice crystals formed in the wake of an aircraft

direct aid   the use of mechanical devices in rock climbing in order to ascend very difficult places

entomologist	a specialist in the study of insects
escarpment	a steep cliff face formed by faulting. The east face of the Sierra Nevada is one of the great escarpments of the world.
exfoliation	peeling off of the outer layers of a curved rock surface, the process by which the rounded domes of Yosemite were originally formed
fault	a fracture in the earth's crust caused by earth movements, resulting in displacement along the break in an up and down direction
free climb	a climb without direct aid; ropes, etc. may be used for security only
fry	very small or recently hatched fishes
full lotus position	a sitting position with legs and arms folded across each other, assumed in Hindu and Buddhist meditation
geomorphology	the study of land forms and how they evolved
glissade	a controlled slide down a steep snowbank, much used in the Sierra when warm days soften the snow
gow	the main dish of a backpacker's evening meal. City people would call it a casserole, and it may contain almost anything.
heliotroper	in this book refers to a person who uses the sun to orient by, in surveying by triangulation
hoof and mouth disease	a highly infectious disease that affects both wild and domestic grazing animals and usually results in the death of the animal
horn peak	a sharp mountain peak formed by the quarrying action of glaciers that erode back all sides of the mountain until only the sharp peak remains; e.g., Cathedral Peak
hydrographic engineer	a person who studies and maps the position and flow of bodies of water above and under ground for the purpose of controlling them
igneous	refers to rock such as granite or basalt formed by the cooling of once-molten material
inholding	a privately held area surrounded by public land, in this case, by national park
kayak	in the Sierra, a rigid wooden or metal box used as a saddlebag on pack animals
larva	the often wormlike form of a newly hatched insect before it undergoes metamorphosis and grows wings
latía	roof beams laid perpendicular to the ridgepole in southwest architecture

lepidopterist	a specialist in the study of butterflies and moths
living glacier	a glacier which is still moving, however slightly; opposite of a stagnant glacier which is essentially an ice field in the process of melting off and disappearing
lode	a vein or deposit of a valuable ore enclosed in a rocky or earthy matrix
metamorphic rock	rock, originally either igneous or sedimentary, which has been chemically and physically altered by heat and pressure and become more compact and more crystalline
metasedimentary deposits	deposits laid down as sediments which were later metamorphosed
midden	a refuse heap from a prehistoric settlement, very useful to archeologists in revealing tools, diet, and habits of the people who left it
monoculture	the cultivation of a single crop over a large area
moraine	an accumulation of boulders, stones, etc., deposited by a glacier
obsidian	volcanic glass, usually black, used by the Indians for arrowheads and other tools
piton	a metal spike with an eye or ring at one end through which to pass a rope; used in climbing
pumice	porous lightweight volcanic rock
pupa	the resting form of an insect which is changing from larva to adult
roche moutonée	a portion of bedrock which has been smoothed on the uphill side by a glacier and plucked on the downhill side so that it seems to resemble a grazing sheep
Sequoia gigantea	the Big Tree or Sierra Redwood
serac	a mass of ice broken off the main body of a glacier which remains standing among the crevasses
sun cup	a depression in the snow at right angles to the sun that deepens as the summer progresses; characteristic of Sierra snow fields with their cold nights and intense summer sun, resulting in daily freezing and melting of the crust
switchback	a hairpin curve on a road or trail
triangulation	surveying by means of triangles
vibram	hard composition soles with characteristic indentations that facilitate climbing on rock or snow; have replaced nailed boots in modern mountaineering

PRINCIPAL SOURCES AND
FURTHER READING

General References

Bingaman, John W. *Guardians of the Yosemite: A Story of the First Rangers.* Lodi, CA: End Kian Publishing Co., 1961. Second printing 1970.

Brooks, Paul. *Speaking for Nature: How Literary Naturalists from Henry Thoreau to Rachel Carson Have Shaped America.* Boston: Houghton Mifflin Co., 1980.

Farquhar, Francis P. *History of the Sierra Nevada.* Berkeley: University of California Press, 1965.

Gilliam, Ann, ed. *Voices for the Earth: A Treasury of the Sierra Club Bulletin.* San Francisco: Sierra Club Books, 1979.

Johnston, Verna R. *Sierra Nevada.* The Naturalist's America. Boston: Houghton Mifflin Co., 1970.

Peattie, Donald Culross. *The Sierra Nevada: The Range of Light.* Edited by Roderick Peattie. New York: The Vanguard Press, 1947.

Russell, C. P. *One Hundred Years in Yosemite.* Yosemite National Park, CA: Yosemite Natural History Association, 1968.

Sanborn, Margaret. *Yosemite: Its Discovery, Its Wonders, and Its People.* New York: Random House, 1981.

Storer, Tracy I. and Usinger, Robert L. *Sierra Nevada Natural History: An Illustrated Handbook.* Berkeley: University of California Press, 1963.

Chapter 1: First There Was a Meadow

Hill, Mary. *Geology of the Sierra Nevada.* Berkeley: University of California Press, 1975.

Matthes, François. *Geologic History of the Yosemite Valley.* Professional Paper No. 160, U.S. Geological Survey, 1930.

149

Chapter 2: Then There Were Indians

Barrett, S. A. and Gifford, E. S. *Miwok Material Culture*. Milwaukee Public Museum Bulletin, Vol. 2, March 1933.

Bennyhoff, James A. "An Appraisal of the Archeological Resources of Yosemite National Park." *University of California Archeological Survey*, 1956.

Godfrey, Elizabeth H. *Yosemite Indians*. Yosemite Natural History Association. Rev. by James Snyder, c. 1973.

Davis, Emma Lou. "An Ethnography of the Kuzedika Paiute of Mono Lake, Mono County, California." Miscellaneous Paper No. 8, University of Utah, Department of Anthropology, *Anthropology Papers* 75:1-55. Photocopy in Yosemite Park Research Library.

Fletcher, Thomas Christopher. "The Mono Basin in the Nineteenth Century: Discovery, Settlement, Land Use." Thesis, MA degree in geography, University of California, Berkeley, 1983.

Heizer, R. F. and Whipple, M. A. *The California Indians: A Source Book*. Berkeley and Los Angeles: University of California Press, 1951.

_____. *They Were Only Diggers*. Ramona, CA: Ballena Press, 1974. (P.O. Box 711, Ramona, CA)

Taylor, Mrs. J. H. (Rose Schuster). *The Last Survivor*. San Francisco: Johnck and Seeger, 1932.

Chapter 3: Then Came the Soldiers

Bunnell, Lafayette. *Discovery of the Yosemite*. Golden, CO: Outbooks, 1980. Reprinted from *Discovery of the Yosemite and the Indian War of 1851 Which Led to That Event*, first published in 1880 by Lafayette Bunnell. Available from Outbooks, 217 Kimball Ave., Golden, CO 80401.

Chapter 4: And Miners

Hubbard, Douglass. *Ghost Towns of Yosemite*. Fresno, CA: Awani Press, 1958.

Trexler, Keith A. *The Tioga Road*. Yosemite National Park, CA: Yosemite Natural History Association, 1961. Reprint 1975.

Chapter 5: Geologists: The Whitney Survey

Brewer, William H. *Up and Down California in 1860-1864*. Berkeley: University of California Press, 1949.

King, Clarence. *Mountaineering in the Sierra Nevada*. Lincoln, NE: University of Nebraska Press, 1970. Reproduced from the 1872 edition published by James R. Osgood and Company, Boston.

Wilkins, Thurman. *Clarence King: A Biography*. New York: The Macmillan Co., 1958.

Chapter 6: John Muir Arrives

Engberg, Robert and Wesling, Donald, ed. *John Muir to Yosemite and Beyond: Writings from the Years 1863 to 1875.* Madison: University of Wisconsin Press, 1980.

Muir, John. *My First Summer in the Sierra.* Dunwoody, GA: Norman S. Berg, Publisher. (Copyright 1911 by John Muir)

Sargent, Shirley. *John Muir in Yosemite.* 2d ed., rev. Yosemite, CA: Flying Spur Press, 1971. (P.O. Box 278, Yosemite, CA)

Wolfe, Linnie Marsh. *Son of the Wilderness: The Life of John Muir.* Madison: University of Wisconsin Press, 1945.

Chapter 7: Joseph Le Conte and the University Excursion Party

Armes, William Dallam, ed. *The Autobiography of Joseph Le Conte.* New York: D. Appleton and Co., 1903.

Le Conte, Joseph. *A Journal of Ramblings Through the High Sierra of California by the University Excursion Party.* 1875. Reprint. New York: Sierra Club/Ballantine Books, 1971.

Chapter 8: The Sheepherders' Invasion

Austin, Mary. *The Flock.* Boston and New York: Houghton Mifflin Co., 1906.

Douglass, William A. and Bilbao, Jon. *Amerikanuak: Basques in the New World.* Reno, NV: University of Nevada Press, 1975.

Langley, Howard. "Mountain Trips: What to Take and How to Take It." *Sierra Club Bulletin* Vol. II, No. 1. (January 1897)

Manson, Marsdon. "Observations on the Denudation of Vegetation: A Suggested Remedy for California." *Sierra Club Bulletin* Vol. II, No. 6.

Paris, Beltran (as told to William A. Douglass). *Beltran: Basque Sheepman of the American West.* Reno, NV: University of Nevada Press, 1979.

Sampson, Alden. "The Aftermath of a Club Outing." *Sierra Club Bulletin* Vol. VI (June 1907).

Chapter 9: Shelley Denton's Caper

Denton, Shelley Wright. *Pages from a Naturalist's Diary.* Arranged by his daughter, Vanessa Denton. Boston: Alexander Printing Co. (Copyright 1949 by Vanessa Denton)

Chapter 10: John Lembert and the Soda Springs

Colby, Will. "John Lembert." *Yosemite Nature Notes* Vol. XXVIII, No. 9. (September 1949).

Garth, John S. and Tilden, J. W. "Yosemite Butterflies: An Ecological Survey of the Butterflies of the Yosemite Sector of the Sierra Nevada, California." *Journal of Research on the Lepidoptera*, July 1963. (1140 W. Orange Grove Ave., Arcadia, CA)

"Obituary of John B. Lembert." *Entomological News* Vol. 7: 224. (September 1896)

Chapter 11: John Muir Returns and the Yosemite High Country Becomes a National Park

Fox, Stephen. *John Muir and His Legacy: The American Conservation Movement*. Boston and Toronto: Little, Brown and Co., 1981.

Muir, John. *The Mountains of California*. The Natural History Library. Garden City, NY: Anchor Books, Doubleday and Co., Inc., 1961.

Sargent, Shirley. *John Muir in Yosemite*. 2d ed., rev. Yosemite, CA: Flying Spur Press, 1971. (P.O. Box 278, Yosemite, CA)

Starr, Kevin. *Americans and the California Dream, 1850-1915*. New York: Oxford University Press, 1973.

Wild, Peter. *Pioneer Conservationists of Western America*. Missoula, MT: Mountain Press Publishing Co., 1979.

Wolfe, Linnie Marsh. *Son of the Wilderness: The Life of John Muir*. Madison: University of Wisconsin Press, 1945.

Chapter 12: The Army to the Rescue

Bingaman, John W. *Guardians of the Yosemite: A Story of the First Rangers*. Lodi, CA: End Kian Publishing Co., 1961. Second printing 1970.

Chapter 13: William Keith Paints the Range of Light

Brother Cornelius. *Keith: Old Master of California*. New York: G. P. Putnam's Sons, 1942.

Chapter 14: The Sierra Club Is Born

Fox, Stephen. *John Muir and His Legacy: The American Conservation Movement*. Boston and Toronto: Little, Brown and Co., 1981.

Jones, Holway R. *John Muir and the Sierra Club: The Battle for Yosemite*. San Francisco: Sierra Club, 1965.

Chapter 15: Early Climbers and Surveyors

Brewer, William H. *Up and Down California in 1860-1864*. Berkeley: University of California Press, 1949.

Gilbert, Grove Karl. "Variations of Sierra Glaciers." *Sierra Club Bulletin* Vol. V, No. 1. (January 1904)

King, Clarence. *Mountaineering in the Sierra Nevada*. Lincoln, NE: University of Nebraska Press, 1970. Reproduced from the 1872 edition published by James R. Osgood and Company, Boston.

Johnson, Willard D. "The Grade Profile in Alpine Glacial Erosion." *Sierra Club Bulletin* Vol. V, No. 4. (June 1905)

Muir, John. *The Mountains of California.* The Natural History Library. Garden City, NY: Anchor Books, Doubleday and Co., Inc., 1961.

Roper, Steve. *The Climber's Guide to the High Sierra.* San Francisco: Sierra Club Books, 1976.

Roth, Hal. *Pathway in the Sky: The Story of the John Muir Trail.* Berkeley: Howell-North Books, 1965.

Solomons, Theodore F. "The Beginning of the John Muir Trail." *Sierra Club Bulletin* Vol. XXV: 28ff. (1940)

Voge, Hervey, ed. *A Climber's Guide to the High Sierra.* San Francisco: The Sierra Club, 1954.

Chapter 16: Colby and Parsons Blaze a New Kind of Trail: The Sierra Club Outings

Eells, Alexander G. "In Tuolumne and Cathedral Cañons." *Sierra Club Bulletin* Vol. IV, No. 1. (January 1902)

Hutchinson, J. S., Jr. "Camp Commissariat." *Sierra Club Bulletin* Vol. III, No. 2. (May 1900)

Langley, Howard. "Mountain Trips: What to Take and How to Take It." *Sierra Club Bulletin* Vol. II, No. 1 (January 1897)

Parsons, E. T. "The Sierra Club Outing to Tuolumne Meadows: A Man's View." *Sierra Club Bulletin* Vol. IV, No. 1. (January 1902)

Parsons, Marion Randall. "Will Colby's Last High Trip." *Sierra Club Bulletin*, 1930.

Randall, Marion. "Some Aspects of a Sierra Club Outing." *Sierra Club Bulletin* Vol. V:221ff. (1904)

Sexton, Ella M. "Camp Muir in the Tuolumne Meadows: A Woman's View." *Sierra Club Bulletin* Vol. IV, No. 1. (January 1902)

Chapter 17: The Sierra Club Buys the Soda Springs, Loses Hetch Hetchy, and Builds Parsons Memorial Lodge

Cardwell, Kenneth H. *Bernard Maybeck: Artisan, Architect, Artist.* Santa Barbara: Peregrine Smith, Inc., 1977.

Fox, Stephen. *John Muir and His Legacy: The American Conservation Movement.* Boston and Toronto: Little, Brown and Co., 1981.

Jones, Holway R. *John Muir and the Sierra Club: The Battle for Yosemite.* San Francisco: Sierra Club, 1965.

Muir, John. "The Hetch Hetchy Valley." *Sierra Club Bulletin* Vol. VI:211-220. (January 1908)

O'Neill, Elizabeth. "Parsons Memorial Lodge." *Sierra*, September 1978.

Chapter 18: Grinnell and Storer: The Birds and the Beasts

Burt, William H. and Grossenheider, Richard P. *A Field Guide to the Mammals.* Boston: Houghton Mifflin Co., 1952, 1964.

Gaines, David. *Birds of the Yosemite Sierra: A Distributional Survey.* Copyright 1977 by David Gaines.

Grinnell, Joseph and Storer, Tracy Irwin. *Animal Life in the Yosemite.* Berkeley: University of California Press, 1924.

Johnston, Verna R. *Sierra Nevada.* The Naturalist's America. Boston: Houghton Mifflin Co., 1970.

Orr, Robert T. *The Little-Known Pika.* New York: Macmillan Co., 1977.

Peterson, Roger Tory. *A Field Guide to Western Birds.* Boston: Houghton Mifflin Co., 1966. Second ed., revised and enlarged, 1969.

Stebbins, Robert C. *A Field Guide to Western Reptiles and Amphibians.* Boston: Houghton Mifflin Co., 1966.

Storer, Tracy I. and Usinger, Robert L. *Sierra Nevada Natural History: An Illustrated Handbook.* Berkeley: University of California Press, 1963.

Chapter 19: Steve Mather Buys the Tioga Road and Throws a Party

Shankland, Robert. *Steve Mather of the National Parks.* Knopf. Second ed., revised and enlarged, 1954.

Chapter 20: François Matthes Reads the Rocks and the Nature Guides Tell the Story

Fryxell, Fritiof, ed. *François Matthes and the Marks of Time.* San Francisco: Sierra Club, 1962.

Matthes, François Emile. *Geologic History of the Yosemite Valley.* Professional Paper No. 160, U.S. Geological Survey, 1930.

Matthes, François Emile. *The Incomparable Valley: A Geologic Interpretation of the Yosemite.* Edited by Fritiof Fryxell. Berkeley: University of California Press, 1950.

Chapter 21: The Twenties in the Meadows

Bingaman, John W. *Guardians of the Yosemite: A Story of the First Rangers.* Lodi, CA: End Kian Publishing Co., 1961. Second printing, 1970.

Cahn, Robert, "Ansel Adams, Environmentalist." *Sierra*, May/June 1979.

Sargent, Shirley. *Yosemite's High Sierra Camps.* Yosemite, CA: Flying Spur Press, 1977.

Shankland, Robert. *Steve Mather of the National Parks.* Knopf. Second ed., revised and enlarged, 1954.

Chapter 22: Carl Sharsmith, The Meadows' First Ranger Naturalist

Sharsmith, Carl. "Comments on the Naturalist Work at Tuolumne Meadows." *Yosemite Nature Notes* Vol. X:73-4. (September 1931)

Sharsmith, Carl. "A Contribution to the History of Alpine Flora of the Sierra Nevada." Ph.D. thesis at the University of California, Berkeley, 1940.

Sharsmith, Carl. Unpublished autobiographical sketch, and personal communications.

Chapter 23: More Tales of the Thirties

Clausen, Jens. "The Harvey Monroe Hall Natural Area." Carnegie Institution of Washington, Dept. of Plant Biology, Stanford, CA, Pub. No. 459.

Clyde, Norman. *Norman Clyde of the Sierra Nevada: Rambles Through the Range of Light.* (Twenty-nine essays on the mountains by Norman Clyde, Foreword by Francis Farquhar and Prologue by Jules Eichorn, with a long letter from Smoke Blanchard.) San Francisco: Scrimshaw Press, 1971.

Presnall, C. C. "Yosemite's Winter Wilderness." *Yosemite Nature Notes* Vol. X: No. 4:33ff. (April 1931)

Rose, Eugene A. *High Odyssey.* (The first solo winter assault of Mount Whitney and the Muir Trail area, from the diary of Orland Bartholomew and photographs taken by him.) Berkeley: Howell-North Books, 1974.

Starr, Walter A., Jr. *Guide to the John Muir Trail and the High Sierra Region.* San Francisco: Sierra Club, 1967.

Chapter 25: The Turbulent Sixties and Seventies

Carson, Rachel, *Silent Spring.* Boston: Houghton Mifflin, 1962.

Eissler, Fred. "Pesticide Fallout in Tuolumne Meadows." *Sierra Club Bulletin* Vol. XLVIII, No. 6. (September 1963).

Sharsmith, Carl. "A Report on the Status, Changes, and Comparative Ecology of Selected Back Country Meadow Areas in Yosemite National Park that Receive Heavy Visitor Use." Photocopy in Yosemite National Park Service Research Library. 1961.

Chapter 26: Today and Tomorrow

O'Neill, Elizabeth. "Walking with Carl." *Sierra* Vol. 66, No. 3 (May/June 1981)

155

INDEX

Round Top, Mount, 67
Russell, Israel C., 68
Russell, Lake, 5

Sacramento, 32
Sacramento River, 20
Saint Francis, 137
Saint Helens, Mount, 4
Saint Mary's College, California, 60, 63
San Francisco, 16, 20, 32, 33, 41, 47, 58, 59, 60, 64, 65, 76, 80, 82
San Joaquin River, 2
San Joaquin Valley, 17
San Jose State University of California, 108
Sardinia, 85
Savage's Trading Post, 10
Scotland, 59
Scots (Scotchmen), 35, 59, 60
Second World War, 119, 130
Senger, Mr., 64
Sentinel Dome, 30
Sequoia National Park, 49, 53, 54, 92, 98
Sharsmith, Carl, 105, 107, 107-9, 114, 119, 120, 123, 124, 132, 134
Shasta, Mount, 105
Sheepherder Lode, 14
Shepherd's Crest (Shepherd Crest), 96
Shields, Allan, 120
Siberia, 5
Sierra Club, 32, 33, 47, 62, 63, 64-66, 73-78, 79-84, 85, 87, 90, 94, 96, 101, 112, 114, 118, 122, 123, 130, 131
Sierra Club Bulletin, 33, 56, 80, 82, 96, 118, 128
Sierra Club Campground, 110, 125, 128
Sierra Club Outings, 73-78, 112, 114, 118
Sierra Club Rock Climbing Section, 114
Sing, Mount, 92
Sing, Ty, 92
Smedberg Lake, 58
Snow Creek, 8
Snow's Hotel, 43
Society for the Prevention of Cruelty to Animals, 63
Soda Springs, 7, 12, 14, 17, 19, 20, 23, 39, 43, 46, 48, 52, 62, 70, 79, 82, 85, 86, 94, 110, 122, 125, 128, 130, 134
Solomons, Theodore H., 71, 82
Soulé, Frank, 29, 30
South America, 35
Southern Pacific Railroad, 53
Southern Sierra, 2, 20, 63
Sovulewski, Gabriel, 57
Spain, 54
Spanish American War, 58
Spiller, J. Calvert, 67
Stanford University, 64, 65, 112
Starr, Walter A. (Pete Starr), 1, 116
Starr's Guide to the John Muir Trail and the High Sierra Region, 1, 116
Stegner, Wallace, 131
Storer, Tracy, 85-88
Stratton, G. M., 70

Strentzel, Louie (Mrs. John Muir), 50
Summit Lake, 24
Sunrise High Sierra Camp, 100
Sunrise Trail, 76
Survey, University of California, 85-87
Swett, John, 60, 62, 63
Switzerland, 17, 19, 105

Tahualamne, 16,
Tahoe, Lake, 32, 99, 108
Tarver, Frank, 120
Taulámne, 16
Telford, Dr. Alan D., 129
Tenaya (Teneiya), Chief, 9, 10, 12
Tenaya Lake, 4, 8, 10, 11, 12, 23, 30, 40, 41, 52, 62, 101, 103, 115, 116, 118, 124
Tenaya Lake High Sierra Camp, 100, 101
Thousand Island Lake, 79
Three Brothers, 24
Tioga (area), 14
Tioga Hill, 14
Tioga Mining District, 14, 15, 40
Tioga Pass, 2, 12, 14, 75, 86, 102, 110, 112, 118, 126, 133
Tioga Road, 12, 14, 20, 90, 91, 92, 110, 111, 115, 125, 131
Trailfinders, 105
Tressider, Mary Curry, 100
Tuck, Charlie, 76
Tulare County, 52
Tuolumne Glacier, 3, 4, 26
Tuolumne Mines, 12
Tuolumne Meadows Lodge, 100, 118
Tuolumne River, 1, 14, 18, 28, 31, 32, 40, 52, 58, 70, 124
Tuolumne River Canyon, 40, 48, 49, 60, 73, 80, 128. See also Grand Canyon of the Tuolumne
Twenty-one Mile Stretch, 110, 124, 125

Underhill, Robert, 112, 114
Unicorn Creek, 134
Unicorn Peak, 1, 3, 114, 120, 136
United States Army Engineers, 67
United States Coast and Geodetic Survey, 67
United States Forest Service, 122
United States Geological Survey, 20, 68, 95
United States National Park Service. See National Park Service
University of California. See California, University of
University of Minnesota. See Minnesota, University of
University of the Pacific, 120
Upper Lyell Base Camp, 18, 109

Vandever, William, Representative, 52
Ventura County, 52
Verret, Dorothy, 125
Verret, Lee, 125, 126
Vernal Falls, 103
Vietnam War, 128
Vining, Lee (Leroy), 11